God
– a balance of probabilities?

A discussion, based on a Philosophical and Scientific balance of probabilities, that provides a different look at Man's relationships with his world and beyond, for those who still have questions.

ROBERT ROWE

© R. B. Rowe, 2012. All rights reserved.

This material is subject to copyright. Except as permitted under copyright law, no part of this work may be reproduced, communicated, published, performed in public, adapted, or modified in any way, without the prior written permission of the author.

ISBN 978 1 921775 76 5

Published by Banro Publishing – 7 Allsops Road, Launching Place, VIC, 3139, Australia. Ph. 61 (0) 3 5964 6914
email: robro27@bigpond.com

*Revised version: Prev epub as "God – without religion"

CONTENTS

PREFACE 9

PART ONE
   The Start of the Journey 17

CHAPTER ONE 19
   Status Quo 19

CHAPTER TWO..31
   Starting Point – Background 31
   Decisions..32
   Historical Aspects...34
   Religions and Creeds – Which One?....................35
   Faith..39
   Introduction of Moral Control 42
   Religious Opportunism 44
   God..45
   Divine Emotions Myth – Love, Wrath, Jealousy, Retribution 46
   Good and Evil 50
   Bodily Resurrection..51
   Heaven and Hell...51
   Religious Elasticity – Free Will 53

Grace 54

Relevance of Religions 56

PART TWO
Old Thoughts – New Thinking 63

CHAPTER THREE 65
Alternative Thinking 65

Back to Basics 68

Terminology 71

Choice of Starting Point 72

CHAPTER FOUR 75
Self 75

Let's Get Personal – You and I 76

The Physical Body 78

The Conscious Self, the Intellect/Ego 78

The Inner Self 80

External Influences 82

Moral Thinking – Conscience? 82

Renewal 85

The Nuts and Bolts of it all 86

Decisions 89

Spiritual Barrier 91

Religious Influence 92

Spiritual World 93

CHAPTER FIVE 97
    Healing 97
    The Immune System 98
    Mind-Body Interaction 99
    Meditation 101
    Background Basics 103
    Existing Medication 106
    Organ Renewal 107
    Death – An Introduction to a New Life? 111
    Grieving 120

PART THREE
    Who Are You? 125

CHAPTER SIX 127
    Spirituality 127
    Life Force – Definition 128
    Man's Self-Awareness 131
    Spiritual Identity 132
    Earthly Relationships 135
    Reason for Spiritual Existence 136
CHAPTER SEVEN 143
    Ethical Considerations 143

Right and Wrong 143
Choice and Chance 144
    a) Environmental Aspects 144
    b) Personal 146
Why Me? 148
Environmental Care 149
Gaia – James Lovelock 150
In considering these matters: 150

CHAPTER EIGHT 153
Relationship with God 153
Need for Religion 161
What Is a Religion? 161
Selective Spiritualism 166
An Overall View 166

PART FOUR
Reconciliation between Science and Philosophy 169

CHAPTER NINE 171
Quantum Theory 171
Scientific Compatibility 172
Nanotechnology 173
Energy 174
Spiritual Energy 181

CHAPTER TEN 183
    Energy Processing 183
    Cyclical Energy 187
    Reality 189
    Concepts of Present, Past and Future 192
    1. Present – The Only True Reality 194
    2. Past – Memory 195
    3. Future – Imagination 197
    The Importance of Memory 199
    Dreams 201
    Thinking Energy 203
    Spiritual Man 206

CHAPTER ELEVEN 209
    Summary 209
    What Now? 212
    Other Spiritual Quests 216
    Afterthoughts 218

MEDITATION 222
    Practical Considerations 222

PREFACE

It is undeniable that religions have created a version of God that suited their particular points of view, based on happenings and occurrences of some thousands of years ago, and that differing interpretations, since that time, have inevitably led to division and confusion for Mankind.

It is suggested here that an alternative and universal view, or understanding, of God is possible if, without denying the value of earlier points of view, we use conjecture based on today's factual understanding.

So, the question posed here is not whether God exists or not – absolute proof of this is beyond us – but rather, whether proof of God's existence can be said to be based on a balance of probabilities, that encompasses us all. Then follows a discussion to try to establish the likelihood of these probabilities.

To do this, the reader is asked to stand aside from religious uncertainties offered over the years by the leaders of the three single deity religions – Judaism, Christianity and Islam – and to examine the subject afresh on a different basis, free of the interpretations that have been inserted by each religion over time.

This requires that we should look for a basis of understanding that has been evident and unchanging since time began, to see if this can provide us with more certain views than before. The only basis of understanding that is irrefutable throughout the universe since the beginning of time is provided by the study of energy.

Now, it seems very reasonable to say that for energy to exist in all of the forms that it does, some intelligent control had to be provided right from the start, and that this is indirect evidence of God's existence.

Consider the following. The universe was formed by the evolvement of energy into various element mixes, which then coalesced into the substances necessary to form the universe and the solar system consisting of the Earth and planets etc.

Basically they are all quantities of energy that appear to us as solid planets, stars etc. because we are set up to see things in this way, so that we can work through our lives to achieve our destiny.

Mankind is also composed of these same elements, and the thought of the creation of intelligent beings, such as Mankind, for no purpose at all seems to me to be illogical and not in keeping with the overall concept of existence – so what is Man's purpose in living?

It could be happenstance, in which case – do we have to develop our own reason for existence in order to justify this existence? The answer to this question is unknown and will probably remain so for time to come, but a moment's thought will confirm that there is a limit to Earth's capacity to support a never-ending expansion of Mankind's physical population. So, perhaps something other than a physical existence should be considered as a logical part of the solution.

In my view, we are spiritual energy beings who have been given the temporary opportunity of appearing in a physical form, consisting of combinations of natural substances, for the purpose of living on Earth, and will revert back to this basic spiritual status at physical death.

A part of the dying process is the elimination of any extreme mental processes we have gathered as physical beings here on Earth. What point is there in these being carried forward automatically to a spiritual realm – they are no longer relevant.

But what about heaven and hell? Well, again, in my view, this is a local disciplinary reward factor promoted here on Earth, to assist in the control of those who follow particular religious views. It's not a consideration – unless you wish to accept it.

It should also be kept in mind that religious scriptures were written by Man to record some happening, of an apparently mysterious nature, in a way as to demand interpretation. This allowed variations in beliefs to suit the individual in charge at that time, or at a later time, as evidenced by the numerous religions and 'isms' in existence today.

For example, the story of Adam and Eve was introduced by St Augustine in the fifth century to provide a convenient and satisfactory explanation of Mankind's origin. But this imaginary exercise was not accepted by early orthodox Christian religions or the Jewish traditions, which felt that it was undesirable for the Scriptures to be read in this way. The story is now considered to be a kind of religious folklore – not seriously accepted or promoted by officialdom, but allowed to be aired, on occasion, as a harmless viewpoint.

It was claimed that the Scriptures were intended as a guide to a way of thinking, rather than as a set of fixed moral teachings or, were to be considered as historically accurate, down through the ages.

Now, because of its intensely personal nature, the decision about the existence of God can't be decided for you by others; you have to make this decision for yourself, probably requiring a degree of simple basic and personal introspection, based on facts as much as possible, free from any artificial religious constraints.

Of course, reaching a decision can be based on a wide reading of philosophical views on the subject, but it must be understood that absolute confirmation is beyond the competence of language or logic. There is always an area of doubt because of incomplete knowledge. It's your choice.

This book endeavours to provide a combined philosophical and scientific viewpoint, based on today's knowledge that is subject to strict confirmation, rather than on outdated stories of the past that were suitable for their times but are just that – stories from the past.

You may find it helpful to join in with other like-minded people to discuss these matters as a group, to arrive at new understandings of our place in the universe. But care should be taken to ensure that extreme views are avoided, and that your views are not being overwhelmed by the majority view.

It's your view which is the important aspect as far as you are concerned, but you should also be prepared to allow others to have differing views, as each of us has our own paths to follow.

All of our views are shaped , firstly, by our education and, secondly, by our experience of life, and this duality of experience leads us to live in two worlds – an Outer world that is, largely, controlled by the rules of Science, i.e. Physics and Mathematics, and an Inner world that is influenced by emotions, feelings, and imagination.

However, these two worlds are bridged by Reason, and it should be kept in mind that without Reason, any discussion about the existence of God becomes meaningless, as God's identity could be decided, according to the individual's personal choice, at any particular time – and changed just as easily. A chaotic and senseless proposition.

So, while the rules of Science can't directly prove the existence of God, it may be considered that, like other continuing facts of life, the evolving existence of these complex rules, based on absolute truths, could be considered as a kind of continuing and unfolding indirect proof that God exists, and, together with Reason, acting as an interpreter or guide, furthers the discussion into the future.

But most of the following points related to what this person or that person is reputed to have said or written, during his lifetime, about his view of God or about the extremes of this or that religion today, and so on. No doubt, many of these comments are important comments but, it might be agreed, they do tend to broaden the discussion a bit by encompassing too wide a range of subjects.

There is no doubt that these are people who gave great thought to the meaning of life and arrived at conclusions that were influenced by their education and ability/opportunity to think independently, and by the conditions existing at that time. In many instances they had to rely on items based on historical fables or wrongly assumed statements or translations etc., and with the benefit of today's hindsight we can see that they may have been in error.

But the important aspect today is not what others think but what do you think? What reason do you have for thinking that God exists? Or not. A viewpoint of the existence of God has to be based on personal conviction with or without the aid of academic teaching, keeping in mind the comments above and the willingness to think about these matters in a meaningful way. Just as we are doing now.

In my view, the likelihood of God's existence can be reasoned into being, but this requires that you become explorers and are brave enough to question and reject those things that are unreasonable, regardless of who said them or proposed them.

Keep in mind, that "a balance of probabilities" has to include the fact that - the concept of an intelligent life force requires a higher intelligence to conceive of it – is this a part of the proof that God exists?

God – a balance of probabilities?

Remember, if something is true, it will be unchanging – if change is apparent then either it's not true, or only true under some circumstances, and this needs to be recognised in terms of its importance to the circumstances as a whole. This is not a new approach – you've been sorting out the facts of living all through your life, and if the truth were known, probably needed to do so to stay alive and well.

The same reasoning process applies to religious or philosophical matters relative to forming a view on whether God exists or not. It is a personal inner search that doesn't require an established religion, although if this is helpful, then fine, but it should be kept in mind that being bound to a religion that promotes tenets that are untrue seems somewhat pointless. Above all you need to be true to yourself.

All social and political questions can be related to given theologies because this is the basis of all thinking through the centuries. But this doesn't necessarily mean that these same questions should be bound by religious limitations today, which, from my point of view, often cloud the issues involved and can be shown to be mainly self-supporting in nature to those very same religions.

You may like to ponder on the thought that, as I see it, Science and Philosophy are two ends of the same stick – each with its own language – feeling their way toward each other at the middle. At this meeting, a common language and understanding will emerge and Mankind will have taken a great step forward.

Indeed, Truth is out there to be found, but requires the application of Reason and Faith, plus a touch of forbearance, to aid in the search.

It should be kept in mind that opinions expressed here, about a complex subject, are for discussion purposes only, and that no offence is intended to anyone or any particular viewpoint. It is hoped, however, that some clarification has been achieved. It should also be understood that, the term Mankind is used throughout this book to denote both Male and Female genders.

PART ONE

The Start of the Journey

The journey of life starts when you are born, but the journey of self-knowledge starts when one realises how little one really knows – Part One discusses the beginning of awareness.

Robert Rowe

CHAPTER ONE

Status Quo

We live and die, to live and die again, in accordance with a process set in place by God.

Now you may question this and it is agreed that despite centuries of research and learned discussion, none of us really know the answer to this question. All we can do is to look at the available facts and these are that, ultimately, we will all die and can only provide guesses at what happens from then on. Hopefully, this discussion may help to sort out these uncertainties.

You will note that I have excluded any reference to religious beliefs in the above comments as these are only factual to those who wish to believe in them. In effect, you are being asked to accept another's truth and, while I respect the individual's choice, it is suggested that the multitude of beliefs in existence is in itself an indication of the uncertainty and lack of ultimate religious authority in this area.

My view is that religions are man-made attempts to provide an explanation of matters over which Mankind had no control and that at that time were beyond his normal comprehension.

Perhaps, then, in the absence of more specific facts, you will agree that a 'balance of probabilities' approach is the best basis we can use to try to sort this out. In reality, life is not only a continuing and unfolding reality to be experienced, but is also a continuing problem of uncertainties yet to be solved. This is the task in which we are all engaged.

Einstein gave us a partial answer that requires an amalgamation of Science and Philosophy – a marriage, apparently, not always favoured by either party. But, because a reconciliation between these two disciplines is necessary to any discussion concerning our existence, you may agree that this book helps to provide a reasonable basis for the inevitable union.

Science acknowledges those matters it can and can't prove, and is in a continuing state of flux in its efforts to widen its boundaries. This is as it should be, but many of the concepts that guide our way of life today just can't be established in the same way – they are, therefore, a matter of opinion or an expression of probabilities until proven one way or the other. Even then, this proof must continue to stand up to the onslaught of later knowledge, or be discarded as irrelevant.

Science is, in fact, a growing body of possible knowledge, some of which we are pretty sure is factual, but all of it is subject to reworking as new knowledge and ideas emerge.

A brief look at our world today shows that since the foundation of the Judeo, Christian, Islamic religions, their more recent leaders, with their overriding competitive and restrictive creeds, have failed in their endeavours to satisfy Mankind's philosophical 'need to know'. We need to know who and what we are – we need to know about our relationships with other species in our world and beyond and the confusion caused by this failure to satisfy Man's need to know has caused our world to go through a critical and very uneasy stage of upheaval over many years.

For example, consider the history of the Holy Wars of the 14th and 15th centuries between Roman-Christian and Islamic faiths and, in more recent times, the persecution of the Jews during the period leading up to and including the 1939–45 war.

Following that upheaval, for example, consider the 60 years or so of competitive religious unrest, resulting in the present unstable situation in the Middle East between Islam and Israel, the divisions within the Christian religions and the worldwide effects on the three main mono-theistic religions.

It is very reasonable, then, to say that this need to know about ourselves is still being held back because just about all of our philosophical beliefs are based on opinions centuries old, which have been given the unassailable 'mantle of Truth'.

The junction where Science and Philosophy meet should be one of cautious mediation, in which both parties can agree on mutual points of view, while accepting that there will always be a shifting area of doubt at the fringe that requires tolerance of the other's standpoint and the realisation that we all gain from such a mutual understanding.

So the question arises – is there an approach that encompasses all of these aspirations and allows a better understanding of our world and its place in the universe? This book suggests that there is another way and outlines such an approach.

A part of this search requires that Man's relationships with his world and his Creator are explored and in so doing, a tentative bridge between Science and Philosophy is suggested. This is the 'need to know' in action and may also be an acceptable starting point for others.

An initial look at the Judeo, Christian, Islamic religions shows that the core basis of these religions is the insistence and reliance on specific interpretations of historical records and precedent for their versions of the revealed Truth. It is suggested here, that the continuing promotion of these differences is the main cause of the confusion now existing in the search for an understanding of Mankind's place in the universe.

This is not restricted to any particular religion or period of time but seems to be a general ongoing malaise that has existed for centuries. For example, in 1616, Galileo's demonstration that the Earth revolves around the Sun was in direct contradiction to religious teaching of the day, leading to his excommunication and to his work being restricted for many years as a result.

Other examples are the religious approval of the Crusades with attendant atrocities, the terrible tortures of the Spanish Inquisition, the Roundhead activities in Britain and the more recent atrocities in the Middle East and Europe. All in the name of God and the individual's particular religion.

It is indisputable that the continuing usage of strict, ancient interpretations of religious texts, written for those times, often many years after the events took place, is questionable. That these original reports were often subject to later translation errors also adds to the uncertainty factor.

For example, a translation of early Greek for the word 'virgin' could also be read as 'young girl' – a very similar meaning. But, consider what this might mean in relation to the concept of the claimed virgin birth of Jesus – although it doesn't, in any way, deny his later lifetime achievements.

Of course, the problem with revealed truths is what to do when, later, it is found that a particular truth was not so infallible after all, and it seems irrefutable that any religion founded on ' truths' which are not true, has to be in danger of irrelevancy. This leads me to four observations:

First, a great deal of wasted effort has gone into trying to prove what has been acceptable and comfortable in the past, rather than examining the subject afresh and making adjustments where necessary. This is still happening and is a part of the malaise referred to above.

Second, most major religions or creeds tend to apportion human emotions to their representation of God, as part of their beliefs, despite the complete lack of proof of this in the light of an unemotional examination of the facts.

Third, is the degree to which religious support is given to seemingly endless and life threatening conflicts, *in the name of God*, to justify particular viewpoints. This is evident in the Middle East, Europe, Asia and the Americas and is not specific to any individual religion or creed. The fact that this support is not strictly in accord with these religious teachings is conveniently overlooked or spoken over.

Fourth, is the strong probability that we are not alone in the universe and if that is the case, then the confirmation of the existence of more advanced worlds will require us to re-evaluate and realign our beliefs and many of our practices (where appropriate) in the light of new knowledge. An example of the complexity involved in this last concept alone is that supposing we accept that there are, say, 10,000 other planets in the universe that can support intelligent life forms, and also accept that the Judeo, Christian, Islamic religions are true. Doesn't this also mean then that we have to allow for the possibility that there are 10,000 other versions of the Judeo, Christian, Islamic story in existence?

Each would be at differing stages of unfolding or fulfilment – some more or less advanced than our own version. Perhaps a different version from our own? More true? Each will be just as true for its inhabitants. So, does this mean that Truth is a variable according to where we live or our specific level of understanding?

If this is so, then what makes our version of the Judeo, Christian, Islamic story the correct one? Wouldn't it be prudent to look afresh at our current spiritual development with this in mind? So, which man-made religion do you think meets with God's approval? Why do you think this is so and, importantly, how do you know? Are you relying on someone else's opinion once again?

The views expressed here may be confrontational, in that I am asking you to accept an unconventional view of Man's place in the scheme of things that not only offers an alternative non-dogmatic approach to living, but also has the advantage of allowing a greater degree of freedom of thought, thereby allowing for new truths as they arise, and providing a continuing level of certainty about our lives.

It will be apparent throughout this book that I am asking you to express your opinion on the various matters raised about the basis for living *your* life, and this is the important aspect – it's your life, what do you think about it all? It is hoped that the result of all this is a more balanced and sensible approach to life, with less fear and superstition to daunt you, and an increased ability to embrace whatever lies ahead.

Some of the views put forward here are similar to those of a group of writers and thinkers who lived during the 17th and 18th centuries and included such notables as Rousseau, Voltaire, Benjamin Franklin, Thomas Jefferson and others.

But as you will see from the following, this similarity just confirms the fact that anyone today can arrive at a better understanding of a more factually based philosophy, if the time is taken to do so. However, we should always leave room for the point that some things just are – we can't know everything. There is always the possibility that we will know and understand more tomorrow and be able to benefit from it, if we have the wit and opportunity to do so.

This work is in four parts and discusses the concepts of the existence of an Inner Self, Mind- Body Healing, Death, Spirituality, concepts of the Past, Present and Future, and proposes a basis for a philosophical and scientific reconciliation. It also suggests that history shows that God, as the Supreme Spirit who has endowed Mankind with an indestructible spirit, is probably quite indifferent to what happens to *physical* Man.

Finally, as all of these matters are interrelated and together are a part of the whole, keep in mind that they can't be dismissed because a particular aspect is inconvenient or nonconformist in its nature.

Part One is a brief reminder of the development of tribal authority, the appendage of various religious beliefs to the tribe, the arrival of Judeo, Christian, Islamic, religions, and the part they have played in developing the world's thinking to date, to illustrate the problem of trying to ascertain the truth of the matter. Finally, in this section, you are asked to step aside from these points of view in order to consider Parts Two, Three and Four.

Part Two explores alternative thinking about the Self, and starts afresh to examine the individual's make-up. It also includes a discussion about meditation, body-mind interaction and healing.

Part Three offers a discussion of a different approach when examining the make-up of the individual and provides reasons for adopting particular points of view or conclusions. For example, is there more to Man than what he sees in the mirror, and given that this is so, what form does that entity really take and who or what is it thinking about this? It also discusses the subject of Death and Beyond and offers comments about the need for grieving.

Part Four looks at the relationship between Science and Philosophy. The concept of a God independent of man-made religions will be of general interest, especially to those who have adopted an anti-religious viewpoint, such as Atheism or Agnosticism, who, if you like, may have a secular sacred view rather than the existing religious sacred views.

In these writings, my task is to look at the world as it seems now rather than as it might have seemed ages ago, and to formulate an overall concept of how it actually operates to function as a living system, taking into account the probability of the existence of spiritual entities and the variables that have to be accommodated from time to time.

It is proposed that the underlying principle of our existence is that the one constant that applies throughout the universe is energy. Everything on Earth, including the Earth itself, can be related to its individual quotient of energy and it is suggested that this is the key to the beginning of an understanding of Mankind's relationship with God.

This viewpoint requires that we venture into a discussion on a wide variety of related subjects to establish the point of view, and your indulgence is required where this seems a bit tedious.

This discussion will include many questions, such as does spiritual energy exist and does it obey the same empirical rules of the laws of physics that we are in the process of discovering, or, is this a separate form of energy with different rules? Perhaps the laws of physics we know are just a part of a greater set of laws yet to be ascertained.

If this is so, then perhaps the concept should be considered that Man is really a spiritual energy being, who has to go through the process and appearance of being born as a physical being as a natural part of the process of changing into a spiritual being at death. This might be considered too speculative, but shouldn't we be looking at our lives with this as an actual possibility, or even a probability? Even if you dismiss this idea as too fanciful, you will probably agree that, on reflection, it provides answers to a few questions that have been problematical for centuries.

Each individual must decide for himself the importance of the matters raised. For example, what's the yardstick by which you will live (and die)? This is a very personal decision that no- one else can make or should make for you. It's your life and you only have one attempt at it, so shouldn't you be giving this much more serious thought?

It should be kept in mind that as these decisions are of fundamental importance to each of us, each person's feelings are the important matter here and each of us has an unknown amount of time left to sort these out. It may be later than you think.

When considering these matters you may feel it necessary to question authoritative statements attributed many years ago. Who said that something was so? How do you know that he said it, or wrote it? Is it based on somebody else's word or opinion that that person said or wrote it? Again, how do you know that this person heard or read these comments? If it's something that was translated from another language, can it be tested today to establish its reliability? The questions seem endless and may not be fully answerable now, but they are there to be considered.

These difficulties are referred to more fully in later pages but it is undoubtedly reasonable to say that if a 'truth' is no longer true then it must be regarded, perhaps at best, as a conditional truth and thus be subject to change. It cannot be a part of the yardstick referred to above.

You may also agree that it is quite reasonable to ask where are the writings of recent confirmed conversations between God and Mankind. Is this a measure of Man's progress, that he has lost his ability to communicate at this level, or has God decided to sit back and leave him to be responsible for his own destiny?

So, with all of this in mind, am I saying that all tenets of religions are false? No, but what I am saying is that Mankind's greed for power over the centuries has muddied the waters to the extent that no-one really knows the answers.

While existing religions have served their original purpose of promoting the concept of the existence of a greater power than Mankind, we should now reassess these and base our decisions on the most reliable basis we have – that is, of reason and implications based on true knowledge. It is the individual's responsibility to carry this out as much as he is able.

Robert Rowe

CHAPTER TWO

This chapter briefly discusses the existing position relative to religious beliefs. In addition to highlighting how these have failed Mankind, it discusses how commonly held myths and dogma, in the main, serve to support existing religions rather than the advancement of Mankind's knowledge of his Creator and his spiritual heritage.

Starting Point – Background

It seems reasonable to begin by establishing what we are trying to achieve, or where the discussion is likely to take us. In this instance, the task can be fairly easily defined as a search for the truth of Man's being, his relationship with his world and by extension the universe and, perhaps, his God.

Our path to reach this destination is not easily predetermined and to some degree seems to depend on personal background and experience. It is subject to many diversions and detours, but unfolds as progress is made. The important point here is that you should start thinking about your place in the scheme of things, and avoid continuing to make choices based on half truths that are obviously irrelevant today.

It should also be clearly understood that the existence of many past civilisations is not in question. The written history of these is confirmed by the physical exploration of these worlds to date. They are a fact – we can go there and prove it for ourselves. But what we can't prove are the expressed religious views of those who lived in these worlds at that time.

These have been written in the main as somebody else's recollection of events that happened many years previously, and were maybe translated two or three times since, until today we have a mixture of beliefs that are open to debate.

For example, this has led to a fragmentation within the Judeo, Christian, Islamic religions into various sects, each determined to be the true voice of their particular version of God – often to the point of self-destruction of their own members and other believers.

This is Mankind's dilemma today – what is the truth and how do we establish it beyond reasonable doubt? It may well be that as far as the Judeo, Christian, Islamic religions are concerned, their debate is really about the correct pathway to be chosen, rather than whether God exists or not. If this is so, then this 'pathway debate' is a matter of opinion and a side issue to the main thrust. Certainly, it is not a part of the discussion here. The following chapters provide a brief historical overview of religious viewpoints, simply to form a base from which further exploration can take place.

Decisions

It is understood that this process may be confronting at various stages and at these times one's Intellect either allows this type of exploration to proceed, or dismisses the subject and returns to safer and more familiar ground. In this regard, the fact that you do proceed suggests that you are prepared to consider that previously held beliefs might not be acceptable now. This is an important decision to make because it means that you are open to spiritual growth – but not necessarily of a religious kind.

For many centuries, uneducated and unquestioning Man had little option but to accept the dogma and tenets given to him by local religious authorities, and while these may have been suitable for their time, I suggest that they may no longer be an acceptable basis for today's living.

For example, if part of your rationale in support of something is to say that the Bible tells us ..., or the Koran clearly states ..., or similar ancient writings from the Torah show us ..., then you are still locked into the old doctrinal, antagonistic way of thinking. These inbuilt, self- promoting, 'I am right' parameters, as in the past, will limit further progress.

This is not to say that those particular teachings were wrong for their time, or are completely incorrect now, but we should always recognise that, even in this field, specialist opinions or interpretations are just as likely to be open to human error and bias as any other person's opinion. Beliefs are either true or should show a high probability of being true to be acceptable, and unless of a technical nature, should be able to be expressed simply and not require special knowledge, or be the preserve of specialists, to interpret.

Truth largely depends on the understanding of the seeker and can, therefore, be a variable over time, and as understanding grows so the truth becomes more whole. However, it must be emphasised that what we regard as truth has to be constantly examined to measure it against current facts and has to be amended as necessary. This suggests that the search may never really be over, because this would mean that there is nothing left to be discovered and we will have arrived at the ultimate truth of everything – a somewhat daunting thought.

It will be seen then that this process really clears the way for recognition and contemplation of the greatest mystery of all – the truth of the existence of the human spirit and its Creator. All else then falls into position and our place in the world becomes clearer.

Historical Aspects

Even a superficial look at religious history must bring the conclusion that most religions have been mainly self-serving in nature, and there is little doubt that they are one of the main causes of most wars that Mankind experiences. However, religious history has been well covered by the work of scholars of all faiths and as there is little value in repeating this material, my discussion proposes a different approach.

During the thousands of years that Man has existed, he has evolved from a being who just satisfied his immediate needs for food, safety, shelter and so on, to a being who has developed the intelligence to wonder about himself, the how and why he came to be in existence, the meaning of it all, and what his future might involve.

This ability to be involved in abstract thought is probably one of the basic reasons why Man has survived and it has led to a sense of an awareness of the Self, that is the ability to consider that there may be an entity within that just might continue to 'live' after the physical body no longer exists, and if so then what this might entail.

In more recent years, the main cause of this development has been a general continuing dissatisfaction with the contradictory nature of religious explanations offered by those in authority. These often failed to account for the complexities of daily life and Man, therefore, sought to find other reasons to explain his situation. As you might imagine, this independent thinking was considered 'heresy' and threatening by those in authority, and repressive action was taken to put down any troublemakers.

It is fitting, then, to acknowledge that the basis of our society today is the result of the thinking of those who prepared the way for us – often at great peril. An obvious statement, I know, but one that should be kept in mind when considering a work of this kind, because all of us are the result of this developmental story and have a personal responsibility to carry this forward to the best of our individual abilities.

Religions and Creeds – Which One?

Whilst Man has felt able to combat physical dangers to a great degree, he has not had the same confidence in looking after his own best interests from a spiritual point of view. He was afraid of the inexplicable happenings that occurred and being aware of his inadequacy in this area, was constantly seeking protection from unseen and improbable terrors.

These emotional needs provided a ready haven for those who claimed to be able to offer that protection, and Religions were formulated that tapped into Man's emotional needs, which are both his strength and his weakness. Strength, in that if your message is accepted by Man's Intellect, he will endure much hardship to support this message, and weakness, in that he can be deceived into supporting uncertain causes to his detriment.

There are many religions and creeds which claim to have some special knowledge of the correct path that Man should follow but, in the main, these are supported by books written by Man himself and are his perceptions or interpretations of history at a particular time. It is very reasonable to say that these writings may have been coloured by what a particular man (or men) wanted to accept had happened, or what was felt would be acceptable to his audience (or the authorities?) at that time. In many instances, these were written many years after particular events took place and were often subject to translation from another language. As an example of the problems this could cause, consider the following.

The Old Testament was written in Hebrew – supposedly the language that God used to communicate with the early prophets and which is still in use today. This raises the point as to why God would need to speak at all – he could plant an understanding, or an idea, in a prophet's mind without speech. Of course, this raises the point about how that prophet would know that it was God speaking and not a figment of his imagination?

However, the New Testament was written in Greek from Aramaic sources and in this regard it should also be kept in mind that in the ancient world religion and politics were inextricably intermingled, so fact and fiction are often hard to sort out. Later translations have complicated the picture further.

God – a balance of probabilities?

The Jews of that time were constantly seeking to understand their situation and many sects arose, including those who became followers of Jesus and formed their own versions of what was happening during those times. The Christian Church then separated itself from its Jewish past and held that there was an Old Testament that related to the Jews, and a New Testament that related to the Christian Church, and it is suggested that, in effect, the twelve Apostles were probably a substitution for the twelve tribes of Israel.

Some of the problems referred to, relate to the reliability of the sources of information provided, for example – if Jesus was alone when he was tempted in the wilderness, how can the Scriptures, written many years later, know about this? Hearsay? Somebody's opinion?

Again, it is said that Jesus was alone when he prayed in the garden of Gethsemane, so how does Luke, for example, know the details of this. It's not mentioned anywhere that Jesus offered this information, and because of the deeply personal nature of these occasions, it's probably unlikely that he would do so. So, is Luke's contribution hearsay too?

There are detailed accounts of the crucifixion in all four Gospels, but as the disciples had fled from the scene, where did this information come from, and how would the disciples know of this and also be aware of what Pilate and the Roman soldiers did at that time? Perhaps you will agree that it's reasonable to say that the Gospels were at least partly based on hearsay – hearsay that was to be used as a part basis for the Christian faith.

The early Christian Church gradually evolved into the Catholic version because of its ability to impose its beliefs on its adherents and to set itself apart – the Gospels and a belief that Jesus died on the cross and subsequently ascended into heaven were adopted as factual. This belief is held as a matter of faith, which of course eliminates any consideration of logic as a part of any discussion, and any view to the contrary was deemed heresy.

Again, in referring to the New Testament, there is quite a degree of doubt about who wrote the various Gospels and it is claimed that, as the disciples Matthew, Mark, Luke and John were fishermen, it is very likely that they were illiterate, and that the Gospels were written by Greek scholars who may have put their own 'slant' on what they thought was required.

It seems that Mark's Gospel is based on the Apostle Peter's preaching, and that Matthew's Gospel was probably written by a Jewish Christian from Syria. The author of the Gospel of John is unknown as it was written around the year 100 AD, that is, 100 years after the events portrayed took place, so you will probably agree that there is some room for error in these various writings. So, accuracy of content and confirmation of authorship constitute real problems.

The fact that competing religions and creeds are still in existence, are self-serving in nature and still tend to vigorously maintain the status quo of over a thousand years ago, seems to me to offer sufficient evidence of the lack of absolute authority of these interpretations or claims.

This leaves them open to doubt and question – not complete denial, but subject to new and more factual interpretation and understanding, as seems fit.

Now, it should be understood that the historical existence of Jesus, Mohammed, and other Prophets listed in the various Holy Books is not questioned, but the claimed special relationship with God, based on these books, is a matter of opinion.

Faith

Most religions and creeds offer an explanation of the way in which the world and the universe operates, but when variations from fact or difficulties in explanations occur, then acceptance of these views on the basis of faith in the particular religion's views, or creed, is required. Faith is required to protect them from any lack of evidence, or the appearance of evidence contrary to their views.

A definition of faith could be an acceptance of what is imagined to be true but which can't be proven. In other words, if proof of existence is available then faith is unnecessary. So, it is probably true to say that most religious rites and ceremonies, tenets of faith, are based on someone's opinion of what was required centuries ago, and that these have become embellished through the ages and authenticated by historical usage.

It can be seen, then, that this is faith in what a particular priest or tribal elder said was so, not necessarily what could be clearly established as fact by others, then or at a later time, if they had the ability or opportunity to do so.

Arbitrary customs were also established that became a part of religious views associated with meals, and instances of these can be seen in the dietary habits of Jews, where milk and meat are prepared separately and not consumed at the same meal. This relates back to the need in earlier times for a reasonable way of differentiating Hebrews from pagans, and table customs provided an easy and discreet way of carrying this out.

Again, in more modern times, the need for Roman Catholics to avoid eating quadruped meat on Friday is another example. This is no longer strictly observed.

So these rites and ceremonies were in reality a matter of convenience and opinion, and the opinion, right or wrong, that was going to be accepted was that of the tribal priest or elder in charge at that time. This caused conflicts between rival factions within particular religions, as well as offence to other religions, since they all approached local tribal problems from their own points of view, and answers were, of course, tailored to suit those particular viewpoints.

Similarly, an alternative view of Christianity has been offered, suggesting that there were two factions involved. One was headed by Paul, who some twenty years after the death of Jesus emphasised his view of the mystical nature of Jesus, based on the stories and reports of others. These views resulted in the Christian religion as we know it today with all of its complexities.

The other, apparently, was headed by James, the brother of Jesus, who regarded him as a down to earth revolutionary, more concerned with the overthrow of the Romans and the restoration of a Jewish King on Earth, rather than the accepted emphasis on heavenly matters. This opinion is evidently a part of the translation of the recently discovered Dead Sea Scrolls.

Another point of interest is that the Koran (4:157) in effect offers the opinion that the crucifixion of Jesus was a charade, presumably to assist Roman control over the Jews, but regardless, acknowledges that Jesus should be revered as a prophet in the same way as Abraham, Moses and Mohammed are revered.

So, it is probably fair to say that on more than one occasion creative thinking was used to make answers fit the facts, or facts fit in with the desired answers, and that various concepts were introduced to justify these. But in fairness, we should also accept that such devices might have been justifiable in the light of specific local circumstances existing at that time. However, that doesn't necessarily justify our continuing acceptance of these myths today.

It is also reasonable to wonder, for example, what Abraham, Moses, Jesus and Mohammed would think of what has happened to their doctrines during the intervening years since these were originally propounded. Do you think they would approve of what is now being proclaimed in their names and how this is being put into effect? This is a very real problem and is one of the main causes of most of the world's conflicts today, leading to the justification of all sorts of excesses.

Introduction of Moral Control

As competition for control developed between religious and civil authorities, it became necessary for religious groups to find an area in which they could hold absolute authority.

The concept of sin was then introduced as a means of exercising religious control over uneducated and largely superstitious Man, thus effectively excluding the civil authorities.

The word 'sin' comes from the Greek language and means to miss the mark (or target), but later came to be applied to missing the mark of being a moral person in a general religious sense. Generally speaking, a sin is a moral wrong against the established mores or public conscience of a particular society, but may not necessarily transgress against civil law. It was a troubling concept for civil authorities to cope with, particularly as religious authorities, being the 'official' interpreters of the will of God, had claimed that it was their right to define what was or wasn't against God's laws. It was hard for civil authorities to argue that this was also a part of their jurisdiction.

This situation was welcomed in some societies as it relieved civil authorities from having to make troubling and sometimes self-incriminating decisions, while other societies bitterly resented the intrusion into what they considered to be their preserves of civil control. But it also gave the civil authorities a way of avoiding blame for excesses when it suited them to do so, and a continual state of stress existed between the two authorities.

God – a balance of probabilities?

Freedom from the burden of sin and guilt required the acceptance of the teachings of those particular religious authorities. When they judged that an act was wrong or sinful in God's sight, an opportunity was then provided to relieve the sinner from his guilt by the application and acceptance of a suitable penalty.

Unfortunately, the interpretation of these sins was altered from time to time, to suit particular priestly viewpoints. In some instances this led to the corruptive practice of selling God's forgiveness (indulgences), but regardless of this, if the penalty was accepted by the adherent, an 'official' forgiveness for the sin was earned. This apparently enabled a fresh start to be made because the person involved was, it was believed, cleansed in the sight of God.

However, nobody could produce any real proof that God agreed with this action, so once again we only have the particular priest's word that this was so. But, as an aside, what do you think that God said to these enterprising priests, when they met later …?

The important point here is that superstitious Man allowed himself to be placed in a situation of dependency, and by giving others free access to his innermost thoughts and fears via the confessional, continually reinforced the religious authority's control over him in a way that the civil authorities couldn't achieve. So, in effect, Man has allowed religions to persuade him that the immortality of the Soul was probably theirs to bestow, or at least control, by virtue of their doctrines, but as Man's spirit is already of God and, therefore, immortal and indestructible, their claim is without any real meaning.

Needless to say, Man was discouraged from trying to sort out his spiritual problems on any other basis than by strict adherence to the rulings of that particular religion. Any acts to the contrary were considered as a rebellion against lawful authority, and the crime of heresy, or daring to hold differing religious views, became established.

It should also be kept in mind that those in charge of the civil administration were just as superstitious and subject to the priest's religious discipline as was the rest of the population, and when problems arose they were often caught between two fears: secular, meaning 'off with their heads', or religious, meaning 'hellfire and eternal damnation'. Either way, unless they felt particularly brave or lucky, civil administrators also had to keep their heads down when in dispute with the priesthood.

Religious Opportunism

This religious blackmail allowed opportunities for religious hierarchies to indoctrinate society into providing donations of money, food and lodging for their services, on the basis of acquiring merit in the sight of God. The premise used was that it would help to ensure their salvation in the next world, but the fact that this also helped to enrich the particular hierarchy in this world was, of course, conveniently overlooked.

Perhaps at this point, I should gently remind you of the immense wealth of most major religions existing today. This didn't arrive by chance, but was based on acquisitions by whatever means over the centuries. Society's spiritual welfare became subject to a number of competing religious and civil authorities and history has recorded many examples of property confiscation by both civil and religious controlling groups, each in the name of its own particular brand of authority.

The question of what constitutes a moral wrong was often determined by convenient interpretations by particular religious authorities, as an aid to physical control of its adherents. The fact that there are a number of competing religions, each claiming absolute truth, indicates that none of them have any real authority.

God

In my view, the fact that the gift of life exists everywhere on Earth, in all its forms, is a primary indication that God exists.

It is impossible to describe God in terms that we can fully understand and it may be that God is a living concept, who is personified in the mind of Mankind, by his ability to create and manipulate energy, of which the Universe and all it contains, is evidence.

The question, then, often arises, that, if we accept that the concepts of Time and the Universe etc. were created by God, then what existed before God came into being ?

As Time was created with the advent of the Universe, and didn't exist previously, then, the concepts of "before" and

"after" also can't exist until after the Universe is created. You'll agree that it's very difficult to discuss something that hasn't yet been created, and, of which, there is no knowledge.
It may well be that God is a type of energy able to assume any form necessary for the chosen task at hand and, as far as we can tell, will continue to be so on into the future.

No man can speak for God, but he can offer an opinion on what he *thinks* God's attitude *might be* in a given set of circumstances. But it is still just that: one man's opinion no matter how it is dressed up. Remember that God does not belong to any particular set of religious beliefs, but rather that Man hopes that by adopting specific religious beliefs, he might be more acceptable to God.

The following highlights some common misconceptions offered by Judeo, Christian, Islamic religions about the nature of God, and suggests that these were introduced to support particular religious beliefs and practices of the time rather than to provide an attempt to describe God in any real sense.

Divine Emotions Myth – Love, Wrath, Jealousy, Retribution

A commonly expressed religious view of God is to ascribe such a Being as having human qualities and emotions, such as Father (but not Mother!), love, wrath, jealousy, retribution, and so on, whereas, by definition, God is indescribable in human terms.

All of these emotions are human emotions, probably developed over hundreds of generations primarily to ensure the survival of the young and the family group, and by extension, the tribe and the nation. They provided a basis for

God – a balance of probabilities?

a justification of an individual's disciplinary actions toward others which could be understood by all, at both family and tribal levels. It was the start of an acknowledgement of the importance of relationships between people at a group level.

But to suggest that God has or needs emotions such as these is completely lacking in logic and poses the question – is it really thought that someone as all-powerful as God, overseeing the universe as it were, would need these earthly qualities? If so, then why? Keep in mind that these would be quite unnecessary in a spiritual world.

However, if we look at this from a historical point of view, it will be seen that, as the tribe grew in numbers, the priestly group or caste gathered in strength and developed a selfish survival interest that was often in conflict with the tribal elders' views. It was of advantage that they could offer a stern, authoritative, and protective spiritual father figure as a God who was responsive to their intervention on the tribe's behalf.

This was because a spiritual being with recognisable human traits was the only analogy which could best be understood and accepted by the elders of the tribe, who could see this as an extension of, and support for, their own family tribal authority.

The possibility that a spiritual father figure existed, who exercised his authority over all, seemed reasonable, and also made the prospect of punishment for disobeying this authority (and by inference their own local authority) seem a normal outcome. This was of great value when there was no other readily apparent explanation for an occurrence of some untoward or unfortunate happening. It was the 'wrath of God' punishing the people for some wrongdoing and who could dispute this!

From the priest's point of view, it was essential that his version of God had to be seen to possess recognisable human qualities, because without these, the priest had no basis on which to claim he could obtain special treatment and was out of a job.

But with an emotional God on hand, the smart priest could always find reasons to support a lapse of favour, so that any remaining doubt worked for him and uneducated Man wasn't game to take the chance that God didn't work in that way.

The priest, therefore, secured his own position by introducing the concept that he was the favoured intermediary between the tribe and their God, and only he could seek favours on their behalf. So, an occasional injection of fear plus a type of 'get with the strength' spiel, coupled with a basic knowledge of human emotions, was standard priestly fare.

Further, the priest was able to claim without fear of contradiction that protection after death for the faithful was assured, thus playing on the difficulty and fears that Man has always had when considering an 'after life' existence. This increased the priest's power enormously, because nobody ever came back to disprove his claims – a type of 'snake oil' cure, par excellence.

The chief, who was just as ignorant and frightened as the rest of the tribe about 'things that go bump in the night', was pleased to have somebody on side who just *might* be what he said he was, and just *might* be able to produce the favours required when needed. Additionally, as the priest was the chief's appointee, the chief could bask in the glory when things went well and he had an obvious and ready-made scapegoat if things went badly!

An obvious example of the contradictory nature of the emotional God claim is that, it has to be agreed, it is quite out of character for a loving God to be selective in the choice of which starving infant is to be allowed to live or die, or for how long the suffering should continue. It is also quite unrealistic to suggest that this should be accepted as a religious belief, and/or part of God's Plan – Mankind's plan, perhaps, but belonging to no-one else.

Further, if God is for all people, it is equally out of character that a particular religion should have exclusive rights to favoured treatment. Doesn't this suggest that God is perhaps playing favourites with innocent people? Surely, God would be above this type of pettiness.

Now, the fact that those in most need don't always receive assistance, tends to prove the point that God doesn't have these emotions and that our physical circumstances are really of little interest. It is also just as reasonable to say that the fact that some in need do receive some relief, doesn't prove that God does have these qualities. But it does suggest that, as the assistance received is more often than not a direct result of human concern and intervention, it is an example of Man assuming responsibility – perhaps indirectly – for his own actions and problems.

However, it should also be noted that this does not preclude spiritual intervention, as will be seen later. To suggest otherwise is to deny Man's emotional and spiritual development over the centuries. It seems more reasonable to abandon the attempt to clothe God with human qualities and to place the responsibility for solving our problems on the cause of the problem – Man himself.

Good and Evil

The terms 'Good' and 'Evil' are also man-made, to describe the causes of benefits or otherwise that can occur, and for which no other explanation can be found at that time. To suggest that these benefits or otherwise are divinely inspired, or under divine control in some way, also suggests that God is the source of evil or lack of goodness, or allows this to exist.

This is contradictory unless it is being suggested again that God is, in effect, playing games by applying good or evil to particular men or nations, according to some particular whim. This hardly seems to be the action of a loving Creator, and once again, why would God be interested in these types of trivialisations?

This is not to say that conditions of good and evil don't exist, but rather to suggest that these are opposite extremes in mental attitudes, initially created by Man himself, and subsequently defined by other Men. An evil condition is not a physical sickness – you can't catch a dose of evil – it's a mental condition. If you like, it could be considered a cancer of the mind or of mental processes, and is a term used to describe an extremity of thought which leads to harmful mental or physical practices. It may be the cause of illness but, primarily, it is evidence of a form of madness.

Bodily Resurrection

Another common misconception is the suggestion that a bodily resurrection of a person at some time after death requires the burial of a complete person for later recognition. The physical body is destined to remain as a part of the Earth and its spiritual representation is quite independent of its human condition – alive or dead.

Bodily resurrection is now an outmoded concept and if you give this a moment's thought you will agree that the construction of a spiritual representation of the physical person is quite within the capabilities of a spiritual world if, indeed, this is desirable or necessary.

Heaven and Hell

It is common for religions to offer the possibility of a reward or reprimand to the faithful, to be gained in the afterlife as part recompense for allowing religious domination in this life. Do this or that, mainly what the particular religion espouses, and entry into heaven after death is assured and you are saved.

If the advice is ignored, then entry into hell or some similar state is almost certain, but what does this say about religions that advocate this approach as an inducement to follow their particular beliefs? It plays on fear, ignorance, and superstition, to ensure loyalty and causes followers to experience a continuing and unnecessary sense of fear and guilt with accompanying psychological damage.

Again, the only support for the 'heaven or hell' viewpoint is contained in Man's interpretation of religious history, but this is not to say that, in a sense, heaven and hell don't exist. Rather, it is suggested that these are mental conditions which Man can achieve, according to his compliance or lack of compliance with natural laws here on Earth.

There are many examples of adherents to all religions who claim that they have achieved heaven, or a similar ecstatic state, here and now on Earth, through meditation, prayer, or by some special way of living. Similarly, there are also many examples of individuals who appear to be in some sort of torment, for whatever private reason, that could be thought of as living in a state of mental hell.

No religion or creed has ownership rights to the availability of heaven or hell, and evidence of this is shown by the fact that so many religions use this disciplinary device for their own purposes. They can't all be exclusively right or wrong, but most agree that these conditions can be achieved.

So, human emotions, good and evil, heaven and hell, are more likely to be man-made conditions of mind and the result of Man's own judgment of himself and his actions, not the preserve of particular religions or creeds, as a reward or penalty for their followers. Judgement day then is, or should be, every day.

Religious Elasticity – Free Will

Various devices have been invented to explain inadequacies in these historical arguments, such as saying that God has allowed Man to have free will in order to teach him that: first, when he strays away from that religion's 'true path', he has to bear the results of this action, and second, that he must choose, of his own free will, to follow the true path as interpreted by specific religious authorities, in order to earn salvation in the afterlife.

As an aside, can you imagine the problem of monitoring, say, 6 to 7 billion mental processes, going on throughout the world on a second-by-second basis, in order to sort out who is exercising free will at any particular time? Then, having determined whether any are straying from the true path as defined by various religious authorities, sorting out a suitable penalty, or applying the concept of Grace to excuse them. Sound reasonable?

Now, add all of these up on a continuing basis throughout each life time to arrive at a total, to be considered at the end of each life to decide entry into heaven or hell. Still reasonable? But you haven't finished yet. As God also covers the universe, have a quick look at the number of stars and add in your guess of the population in the rest of the universe, containing millions of stars, for similar instantaneous monitoring. Still sound reasonable? Come on, really think about it.

But closer to home, the free will argument is hardly applicable to those suffering through no fault of their own or without the ability to help themselves, so the question has to be asked, why would a loving God allow this to happen?

Further, why would any man be allowed to cause others to be afflicted because he should be allowed to exercise his free will.

Appropriate and indisputable examples of this would be to consider, in our recent history, the activities of Hitler in Germany, Stalin in Russia, others in Africa, China and S.E. Asia. In even more recent years, the activities of the USA both at home and in the Middle East, and Australia at home, are also open to some criticism in this regard.

Surely a loving God would step in to prevent tragedies of these kinds from happening to all those afflicted and in need, and to suggest that the exercise of Man's insane free will would somehow preclude or supersede God's intervention, sounds like a desperate attempt to support an unsound and insupportable proposition.

Rather, it is considered further evidence that God is not concerned with Man's physical circumstances as these are due to Man's inhumanity to Man, and the solution lies with Man himself.

Grace

In the religious context, grace is considered to be a type of pre-forgiveness for Man's sins because God accepts that Man has difficulty in complying with divine laws and needs a bit of come and go, as it were. This is a Christian belief and the actual definition is the free and unmerited favour of God shown toward Man. This does not relieve Man of exerting his every endeavour to avoid sinning, but apparently provides a safety net for the sincere person, who on occasion makes a mistake and later repents.

God – a balance of probabilities?

If you sit back and examine these ideas, it is hard to avoid the view that priests had to find a way to explain why God didn't behave in the disciplinary way that they had claimed would happen, when transgressions occurred. So, to explain this lack of interest and avoid 'difficult' questions, the safety net ideas of Free Will and Grace were evolved.

This also gave priests room to come back to the individual with 'the carrot of forgiveness' – you've been a bad lad but we can sort it all out for you etc. The alternative for them was a loss of priestly credibility and institutional power of the privileged position they held in society.

But, to take this further – why wouldn't God just make it easier for Man to comply with divine laws instead of making it difficult for him to sort these out, knowing that these will cause problems? What does it prove that God doesn't already know? Why would God bother to go to this trouble to then later have to decide whether or not forgiveness is to be given for those who transgressed? God's plan, again? Really?

Now, if the priest spends a great deal of effort in stressing the dire results of disobedience to his version of God's laws and when these are broken, no retribution occurs, it makes a lot of sense – probably priestly survival sense – to have an 'out' of some sort, doesn't it? The concepts of Free Will and Grace are only necessary if the religious argument is not consistent with logic and the facts.

The assumption, then, that divine emotions exist, seems to me to be a major error, and if these concepts are removed, then the picture tends to become much clearer, as it places the responsibility for our problems back with those who caused them and are in a position to correct them – Man himself.

If you think about this point a little more, and agree that the above is a reasonable approach, you may also conclude that it is reasonable to say that many problems existing today are caused by the forced acceptance of religious concepts, attributed in error to God, that are untenable. When we refer to God in human terms, as being interested in our physical welfare, it really is another way of saying that we haven't bothered to think about the subject very seriously.

A simplification of this is for me to point out that if we place ourselves in a position where we are likely, at some time, to experience a particular problem, we shouldn't be surprised or blame others when the problem occurs. The answer is to continually monitor all aspects of the lifestyle we choose to live, recognise the truth of the possibilities and probabilities and take every care accordingly. This is not a new concept – just a normal commonsense approach to living.

Relevance of Religions

Of course, this simplification has its casualties and means that, in the main, those creeds and religions that depend on man-made hierarchical structures and ceremonial rigidity or strict adherence to questionable historical beliefs or dogma for their existence, are becoming less and less relevant for us.

It is also indisputable that, despite repeated and continuing pleas and prayers for assistance and relief from suffering by religious leaders for many centuries, the same sorts of problems continue to exist. This must cause doubts about the effectiveness of these religions and whether, in fact, their views and claimed relationships with God are really valid: even further, whether Mankind, as a physical race, has ever had a personal relationship with God.

Consider the following. All over the world and ever since recorded history has existed, Mankind has believed in the existence of a greater power and tried to reach this power.

Ceremonies are conducted – sacrifices are made – hymns are sung – donations are made – prayer wheels are spun – holy men rise – kneel – prostrate themselves, and to try to achieve this union, call on Allah, Jehovah, Jesus (and many Saints), Mohammed, and so on.

Each believes that his is the true path and others' beliefs are in error, and to prove it, millions of dollars have been spent, each year, for hundreds of years in killing each other in the name of their particular 'true' God. Shouldn't we stop and think about this a bit more seriously? Do you really think that any religion or belief system is so right – that is, without error in God's sight – that God would be on their side exclusively to the point of condoning the killing of others, and in particular, the killing of others who also profess to acknowledge the same God's existence to the point of worship?

First, such a viewpoint would seem to be an expression of a national religious ego fixation which is provocative to all other religions, and second, there seems to be little real unbiased evidence that it is justified. Isn't this just another example of somebody's assumption of what *they* think God's point of view might be?

Can you recall any instance where it can be claimed without doubt, by all involved, that God has intervened on one side or the other? Perhaps, it might put all of this into perspective if we consider, for example, that during the last 2000 years, each major religion has handed down its version of the true path via some 40 or 50 religious leaders – each accepting that what was told to them was the TRUTH and then, as a part of their leadership tasks, added their interpretations, as they saw it all.

Now, it doesn't matter how sincere these ideas and interpretations were – if the story was questionable right at the start, or these interpretations were just an individual's opinion – where does this leave us? Isn't it obvious, for example, that the God that the three Judeo, Christian, Islamic religions relate to, is the one and same God, and that their squabbles are really about which pathway should be used to acknowledge this Deity? That is, the squabbles are about something which is a matter of opinion anyway? Isn't this a case of concentrating on the shadow instead of the substance?

It is quite evident that religions, with all of their rituals and dogmas, are divisive by nature and, by their need for leaders and an organisation to support them, can't help but promote religious elitism. As such, history shows us that they can only provide a temporary variation to Man's condition.

Most religions require that its adherents have faith in whatever their teachings are and this is all very well and probably a necessity in the absence of facts. But, isn't it also necessary that the individual should explore whatever facts are available in order to establish the validity of what to have faith in? Faith in something which doesn't have a demonstrable factual base of some sort, seems to be quite unreasonable. But what does it say about religions that need to promote hellfire and damnation as an incentive to follow their particular beliefs?

So, the question has to be asked, why do you subscribe to any particular religion if it can be shown that the various teachings contain statements which are not consistent with the facts as we know them today? Further, many of the respective practices now have very little to do with God, but everything to do with maintaining a particular religion's domination.

This is not to just dismiss all of these teachings as completely irrelevant, as many of them form the basis or foundations of our society and way of life today, and should be retained. It is also undeniable that over the centuries, churches and temples of all faiths have been active in promoting the spiritual development of Mankind and, despite their parochial views, are deserving of support from those who wish to accept these teachings.

Certainly, where special advice is needed, then access to religious views may be considered appropriate, but if alternative thinking, as suggested here, is acceptable, there will be a difference. The faithful will no longer have to accept questionable teachings and no longer have to confide their innermost thoughts in the Confessional to achieve salvation – a doubtful concept anyway – and the strict disciplines of the particular religion will no longer be enforceable.

As a basis for this alternative thinking, all religions will need to continually upgrade their basic beliefs to ensure that they remain as factual as possible in the light of current knowledge and remain relevant to the needs and education of the people they serve. An evolving religion based on whatever facts are available and are coming forward, will always be relevant to its followers.

My feeling is that all religions are man-made for their time and place, and once this time has passed, unless they have evolved with the passage of time, they have little relevance except as history. This relevance depends largely on the education of the people it is supposed to serve, and as this improves, so an unchanging religion declines in value to those people. But it should be kept in mind that this does not exclude a belief in the existence of God, if this is the individual's viewpoint.

Changes in education may cause a change in Man's concept of God and, therefore, his approach to God may have to change also. History has shown that as Man has become more educated and able to think for himself, the maintenance of outdated, arbitrary and restrictive practices of some religions has come under question, thus causing increasing irrelevance and uncertainty.

But, it also should be acknowledged that the value of churches, temples and mosques lies in their ability to provide a place and time for the individual to separate himself from everyday affairs and so make it easier for him to approach his God.

God – a balance of probabilities?

So, it seems very reasonable to me that some independent reassessment of the relevance of ancient philosophies is in order, to enable us to measure and adapt religious beliefs to today's conditions on a more realistic basis. This is the reason for the journey on which we all are embarking. Now, to alternative thinking.

Robert Rowe

PART TWO

Old Thoughts – New Thinking

This Part suggests that some old ways of thinking should be revisited and the individual should be rediscovered, by establishing that his spiritual Inner Self exists, and that mind-body healing is possible.

It offers an example of an alternative treatment process in action. It suggests that death is really a new way of life and offers some comments about grieving and the 'why me' problem.

Robert Rowe

CHAPTER THREE

Alternative Thinking

Having placed existing religious beliefs to one side, it is everybody's responsibility to decide on the parameters which will guide them on how to live their lives – it is not enough to leave this to chance. Choices have to be made, unaffected by half truths and outmoded opinion as much as possible.

This is not to suggest that a fixed dogmatic viewpoint of any kind should be adopted, but rather that each person should endeavour to form a realistic view of themselves and of their beliefs and changing needs, and of the society in which they live, that is as factually based as possible.

Further, they should try to develop an overall general understanding of how Science, a factual explanation of how our world exists, and Philosophy, a theoretical search of ideas, might fit together as a whole, as a basis for living in today's world.

Of course, in view of the religious confusion existing today, it is reasonable to ask the question, why be concerned about it at all – if the experts can't agree, what chance do we laymen have of sorting it all out? Why not just go with the flow until somebody arrives with some definitive answers and then we can all be saved by the one true religion!

Well, standing aside from this light-hearted approach, a moment's reflection on the discussion contained in previous pages will show what reliance on better qualified people has achieved, and that the 'some other time' approach just ignores two basic points.

First, the reasons why this book was written in the first place, and second, that each person's available time to carry out such a review is quite unknown. Perhaps these reasons should be restated.

Doesn't it get back to whether, as a reasonably well educated society, trying to understand the philosophical basics about our existence is important or not? Yes, of course we can ignore the whole deal, as suggested above, but is this good enough?

Well, it's your choice, it's your life – but, as you have an unknown lifespan, and as Man has inherited a strong inbuilt belief that he has an indefinable Inner Self, and that there is something greater than himself 'out there' that relates to this Inner Self – he has an almost compelling inbuilt need to try to find out what that something is all about.

The recognition of these beliefs and needs is the basis of why most religions have arisen, but priests were more often concerned with controlling the direction of the search, rather than enabling its progress. It may be considered that ultimate failure was predestined for these efforts if only because of the resultant confusing and competing conclusions which came into being – as we can now testify.

God – a balance of probabilities?

It seems to me that the need to simplify and establish our true nature, and how we relate to our increasingly complex world, is of fundamental and increasing importance, because in so doing, we rid ourselves of this confusion and simplify our destination. We also gain an indication of what lies ahead.

So, isn't it better to go forward, basing our thinking on facts or, as near as we can get to facts, rather than on a melange of opinions and rules of doubtful value, handed down to us through the centuries?

While this reduction in control would be frowned on by religious authorities, don't we owe it to ourselves and future generations to try to simplify our spiritual heritage? Don't you think that God would approve of Man making a sincere attempt to clarify confusion? Isn't this a part of Man's raison d'être?

Remember that there are many pathways available to reach whatever you decide is your destination, and that as you proceed and new facts present themselves, you will probably become aware of other options. This is simply the result of becoming aware of changing needs as you grow in knowledge, and while others can offer guidance, remember that it is always your choice, because you are the only one who knows if what is offered is right for you.

You may be surprised at the number of people you will meet on the way who are also engaged in a similar search, and many of the answers you arrive at will also be the same as their answers.

It is hoped that the following discussion might be helpful in sorting this out. Of course, the need for alternative thinking is never really satisfied, and this is as it should be, because new facts and ways of expressing them are constantly appearing. This discussion is just a starting point – an attempt to provide some clarification in the unfolding story of Mankind's existence and his relationship to his world.

However, remember that each of us is a work in progress until we die, and the answers we encounter as we go along might point us to quite different paths from those we thought might be the right way when we started out. So expect your views to change as you proceed.

Back to Basics

Perhaps, as a starter, it should be said that it seems very reasonable to me to accept that the universe was created according to the laws of physics (including those we have yet to discover) as these were put in place by God, and that Mankind evolved after a formative period. Now, whether this included Adam and Eve as created beings in their own right, or as an evolvement from a lesser being, or even by some other process, seems to me to be immaterial, since all of these sources could be a part of the creation process.

What is important is that we are here now and have the ability and opportunity to try to sort out who and what we are and, perhaps, where we are going from here. Debates about creation are not relevant to our discussion. We are concerned with the present and what the future holds for us. The past is only of interest to the extent that it provides some basis to support our search for truth today.

God – a balance of probabilities?

But this is not to ignore Science, as it is also critical that our comments should be constantly checked against any relevant new scientific thinking, and while complete compatibility may not always be immediately available, perhaps because of insufficient information, there should be no direct contradiction in our statements. If a contradiction is clear and unconditional then our standpoint must be altered, regardless of history to date.

Now, because it is impossible to determine the credibility of various religious claims without accepting another's interpretations and experiences, which may be centuries old, it is felt that the best way to start the journey is to sidestep these and go back to self-evident truths that are beyond question now, and can be clearly seen to be true by anyone, at any time.

However, at all times, these truths must be reduced to their bare essentials as much as possible and simply judged on this basis. The question has to be constantly asked – is it true under all circumstances or only factual because of some special criteria? Is it really true or a conditional truth?

Anything that can't be clearly established by an unambiguous demonstration, or by a very high probability factor, should be disregarded as fact, but not necessarily ignored.

For example, we can reasonably say that it is true that the sun will always shine and that gravity will always hold our world in place. This is something which has happened for as long as recorded history shows and can be assumed to have a very high probability factor of continuing to occur each day into the foreseeable future. These can reasonably be relied upon as continuing facts.

But we should recognise, of course, that what we regard as a truth will only exist until it can be disproved and replaced by a new truth or varied in some similar way. This may take thousands or millions of years to evolve in accordance with changing conditions. For example, referring to the sun – the scientific process of evolution requires that our sun, like other stars, will eventually die, and that the effects of gravity will alter.

Our Earth will also die as a direct result, but because of the time scale involved, it is reasonable for us to regard a daily sunrise and the present degree of gravity as a constant fact, even though, strictly speaking, it will not always be so.

Similarly, other occurrences that have a high probability factor of happening again, or can be caused to occur again under given circumstances, can also be accepted as a fact, but should be regarded with some reserve until other factors prove it one way or the other. Until this happens, it is a conditional fact – that is, it requires specific circumstances for it to be a fact.

As it is also obvious that there are no ready-made answers to many of the questions which arise, some conjecture, or opinions based on facts and conditional facts, must be offered in an effort to sort out a reasonably logical framework in which we should work. However, it must always be made clear that these are opinions and subject to change in the light of later knowledge. As always, there are choices to be made.

The first step then seems to be to try to establish a basis for discussion that accepts the past, but puts it to one side without judgment. This involves the acceptance of the fact that there are two truths always in existence. One truth is a relative truth, that is the truth as the individual perceives it here and now, based on experience, education and knowledge of life and, therefore, subject to some variation, while the other is the ultimate truth that is immutable.

These two truths may be the same – but we can only know our relative truth – the truth of what is now a part of the pathway towards the ultimate truth. We can draw some comfort if most others also find that our relative truth seems to be universally acceptable.

The next step should provide a rational, ongoing, general explanation of the relationship between the physical and any other aspects of today's world that need to be considered, including our destiny. If there is no destiny then our discussion ceases to be relevant.

Terminology

This is always a problem as it is often difficult to provide words which adequately describe a meaning or process, because words can have different meanings and weights of meaning to different people.

So, it is of especial importance in this discussion that there is no confusion about what is meant by particular terms or words. It is requested that any terms used be accepted at suggested face value to illustrate the point of view, rather than perhaps any other, or more traditional, value.

An example could be the word 'Soul'. This has been adopted by most religions to help promote their specific religious views, but it really is a word to denote a personal, spiritual, Inner Self, and doesn't necessarily need to have any specific local religious context at all.

Choice of Starting Point

While there may be many starting points, it is considered important that we should try to start with a general proposition that should be easily understood and accepted by all, and then to progress in stages from that point, keeping in mind our requirement to differentiate between fact and fiction.

But reasonable conjecture must always be a part of our discussion, on the understanding that it is there to be confirmed. This will provide the discussion with a continuing integrity within the limits of available facts, but if what is offered isn't considered reasonable, then others may wish to substitute their own thoughts. However, these ideas must also be followed through thoroughly, to establish whether they are any more factual or relevant, taking into account all factors likely to influence the discussion.

In other words, you can't stop halfway just because you are satisfied with the result. You must push a bit further to uncover any other circumstances likely to arise, and continue to test the conclusion accordingly. It may well be, as we become more aware of the ramifications of a particular truth, our viewpoint may change in a number of ways as we proceed. So testing viewpoints is important.

God – a balance of probabilities?

As this matter relates to ourselves, then let's start by describing ourselves, first in a broad, general sort of a way, and second, broken down into various categories as seems appropriate. Again, let me emphasise that any terms used are not religiously inspired, but are used because the meaning is most suited to the discussion. From here we will move into associated areas, as seems fit.

Robert Rowe

CHAPTER FOUR

Self

As Mankind's physical appearance is obvious and requires little comment, this chapter endeavours to define who or what is the entity within – the Self – and discusses a wide range of subjects to do this.

So, who are you? Well, the answer to this obvious question is that the real you is not the description and name by which you are usually known.

For example, when you were born, you were a 'clean slate' as far as conscious energy knowledge was concerned – all of the labels that you now have are additions that have been applied according to your later lifetime activities.

The real fundamental 'you' is a spiritual energy that has access to your mind and manifests itself on the occasions that your intelligent energy allows, and its abilities are only limited by the restrictions that your intelligence applies to it.

If you deny its existence then its activities or ability to assist will be minimal – if you are convinced that it exists then you can call on it to help.

As Mankind is designed to survive on Earth regardless of size, race, colour, etc. and all of us are very similar in our essential physical makeup and needs, it is also reasonable to assume that our spiritual needs, which are awakened at birth as a part of our natural inheritance, will also broadly be the same. Why should they be any different?

This is not to say that everyone's spiritual development is at the same level, or that differing levels of understanding don't exist – maybe for educational reasons, for example. However, once a basic level of understanding is established then Mankind can proceed at whatever level and pace is chosen, free of man-made 'isms' and in-built exclusivity factors. So let's start the process of defining ourselves as a whole, including a spiritual point of view.

Let's Get Personal – You and I

Under normal circumstances, all of us are born equally equipped for life's journey and it's what we make of ourselves that counts when assessing how well we are travelling. This has nothing at all to do with any outward physical appearance or possessions – it has to do with our personal inner view of ourselves and, as we are the only person who knows the full truth about ourselves, this is the true starting point for each of us. This exercise also helps to define what is needed to improve ourselves and, in this regard, anything less is pointless.

So, for our purposes, a human being can be considered as having three parts and it should be kept in mind that each of these parts has one common quality – that, at a very basic level, they are all forms of energy as described by Einstein's Theory of Relativity. This clearly establishes that, under some circumstances, E (energy) and M (mass or physical content) are different ways of describing the same stuff but expressing them in different terms. It is suggested, therefore, that as alternative thinking becomes more acceptable, the concept of an energy view of ourselves and the Earth may also be more acceptable.

1. **The Physical Body** – The body's function and value lies in its ability to provide a safe 'container' for its Conscious Self and Inner Self/Life Force while it is in existence on Earth. Apart from procreation of the species, this is its only purpose, as the body is finally rejected at death.

2. **The Consciousness or Intellect/Self (Ego)** – This controls its everyday activities, keeping in mind that unconscious activities are largely the automatic response part of the consciousness. The Ego is the conscious view of the Self, and it is its misuse in self- promotion that is the cause of many of Mankind's problems.

3. **The Inner Self** – This contains the individual's spiritual component and the Life Force that powers the body physically, and its initial function is to start up the process of the development of the human being at conception, in accordance with the individual's inherited DNA. It can and does on occasion work in conjunction with the Intellect.

It should be kept in mind that each of these parts has one common quality – that at a very basic level they are all forms of energy as described by Einstein's Theory of Relativity. This clearly establishes that, under some circumstances, E (energy) and M (mass or physical content) are different ways of describing the same stuff but expressing them in different terms. It is suggested, therefore, that as alternative thinking becomes more acceptable, the concept of an energy view of ourselves and the Earth may also be more acceptable.

Now, looking at these parts more closely.

The Physical Body

The physical body is obvious, and being aware of our various senses, for now, looking in the mirror can be accepted as sufficient proof that you exist. Of course, if there is no body reflected in the mirror, then you have a reality problem and you'd better fix it quickly!

I'm told that non-reflection is a worry that a new mirror won't fix!

However, for now it is safe to ignore this possibility until it happens, and accept that a reflection is sufficient proof of a physical presence.

The Conscious Self, the Intellect/Ego

It can be clearly established that the body is controlled by electrical energy impulses and it is obvious that we have a Conscious Self/Ego or Intellect (or Body Manager!) that sorts out the task of deciding what functions are to be carried out on a second-by-second basis, and how and when these will occur. These impulses can be measured and logic suggests that there are at least two different forms of electrical waveform energy involved:

    a.   The intelligent waveform energy generated by the Intellect when making decisions, often including the emotions, within the mind – if you like, the thinking/knowing/deciding energy'

b. A different kind of energy which causes physical movement, muscle expansion and contraction and so on – an 'action' energy

That these two energies exist is established by the fact that while a paralysed person's mental activities may remain complete, they are unable to cause limb movement because there is an interruption to the flow of 'action-directing' energy to these limbs.

Normally, together these initiate the activity that follows the decision made by the Intellect and trigger physical action (or not) in the body. While both of these energy forms are extremely important, the intelligent energy is of greater importance as it controls all conscious activities. It also enables creative thinking, including the decision to contact the spiritual energy component of the Inner Self.

Perhaps it might be helpful if we briefly discussed the concept of the Self, or Ego, as our own particular and personal identity – the 'I' person. This is the outward manifestation of the individual's personality or Intellect and overlays all his thinking and actions. It is expressed in all that we do and say, on a daily basis, and enables us – and others – to know ourselves as separate entities.

The statement that 'I am' is a necessary recognition of the existence of a personal Inner Self and is, of itself, no more than this.

But, when the developing conscious intelligence adds labels to the 'I am' statement for self- promotion purposes, problems can arise. For example – internal statements such as 'I am a genius' or ' I am better than this person or that person', for whatever reasons, are simply self- promoting activities that are misleading functions of pride and immaturity that will serve no good purpose.

However, it has to be acknowledged that we may be forced to adopt various external persona in order to carry out our normal living functions, but despite this, our internal idea of this special 'I' person stays the same throughout our lives. It is constant, despite the fact that our external views might change through education and living experiences, age, and so on. Each of us is our own personal, unchanging 'I'.

Doesn't this suggest to you, that this in-built concept of an unchanging entity within us is the *real you*? Not necessarily the 'public you' but the very private essence of you as a physical being. This is the part of ourselves that makes contact with the Inner Self and, in my view, ultimately combines with it to become the Soul after physical death. They are both energies of a spiritual nature.

The Inner Self

Well, as you can imagine, it isn't possible to do other than speculate about this aspect, but logic suggests that at conception, the Inner Self or Soul gives the 'spark of life', the task of forming cells in conformity with our own individual DNA, and imbuing them with a Life Force energy to create an individual human being, that is both physical in appearance and energy in content.

God – a balance of probabilities?

The choice of whether a physical view or an energy view is to prevail is an indication of our mental development as a species, because to enable us to exist on a physical Earth, we are indoctrinated at birth to only regard ourselves as physical entities.

While the concept of a Life Force is easily understood and accepted because the fact is self- evident, an Inner Self or Soul – the spiritual side of the equation – is a bit harder to establish to everyone's satisfaction, as absolute proof can only be assumed.

Ultimately, it depends on the individual's gut feeling that it must be so.

Perhaps the following might be helpful. It is commonly said in conversation that 'I'll give myself a good talking to …' or 'you'd better talk to yourself about …' when debating a matter requiring a difficult decision. When you are musing about something in this way, to whom are you directing your thoughts and seeking an answer from? Isn't this an unconscious reference to the fact that you are going to consult with another entity within – your Inner Self?

Now, I appreciate that this isn't a satisfactory answer, but we are stuck with an apparently insoluble individual emotional problem, and it is, therefore, up to each individual to think about it and decide for himself what his personal views are. Certainly, no-one else can, or should, make this very personal decision for you.

External Influences

It is reasonable to say that since time began, Man has often felt that his circumstances have been ordered by powers over which he had no control, and concluded that an unseen spirit world of some sort existed to explain this intervention. This resulted in the growth of religions of all sorts through the ages, each claiming to be able to intervene in these activities, but, no conclusive proof could be offered apart from that provided by opportunistic happenings.

Moral Thinking – Conscience?

The mind is the mental area where decisions are made concerning very basic matters of importance to the Self. Two obvious examples are the body's physical wellbeing and the maintenance of our own intellectual and personal standards. This is an ongoing and never- ending process that decides who and what we are as individuals.

So, perhaps when considering the Inner Self, some comment should be made about the nature of thinking. Regardless of the trigger, your Intellect is the originator of your thoughts – good and bad. These are constantly under review to enable them to be altered, or not, according to the influences and/or circumstances at that time. It is reasonable, therefore, to say that, as it is your Intellect which directs these reviews, *you* are likely to be influenced as a person by the type of thoughts *you* allow to be considered.

But the Inner Self (or spiritual Self) also has the ability to observe your mind's workings and perhaps influence the thoughts being considered – it is an inseparable part of the essential you and is like an object and its shadow. In effect, the Inner Self competes with the Ego/Intellect, which is mainly focused on the body's physical needs to influence what actions the 'physical you' should take and, therefore, the type of person you display.

It is suggested that the fact that you are a thinking person, capable of thinking or searching along moral lines, and that this happens is further primary evidence of the existence of the influence of a spiritual or Inner Self. That is, that the search is initiated by something in a rational, ordered way, and is the result of other than the satisfaction of basic physical needs such as hunger, thirst, and so on.

Perhaps it should be made clear that in this discussion I am not referring to 'hearing voices' or anything of this kind – I'm speaking about those occasions when you are musing about a course of action to be taken and a different thought or train of thought suddenly occurs. Where do you think this thought came from?

So, let's push this along a bit further. What do you think causes you to think as you do? What influences you to use your Intellect to think those particular thoughts at that particular time and, on occasion, to then apply a moral filter/judgement to make specific decisions. These may not always be supported by logic but it's common for people to say they have a feeling about something. They can't explain it, the feeling or point of view just 'seems right'.

It is suggested that the options are considered logically by the Intellect within the mind and an initial decision is made as the first part of the process. Then, almost immediately, a secondary and separate consideration involving moral aspects is often made. The final decision then depends on the weight placed on each of these decisions by the individual. But who, or what, is it that examines the Intellect's thoughts and then causes a further selection to be made? If it is your Intellect alone that makes these decisions, then surely the moral options would have already been included automatically as a part of the initial decision making process.

Doesn't this suggest that there is another entity involved in making a moral judgment; that is, there is input from another source other than your Intellect to help decide the question? Certainly, it is possible for a number of options to be considered at the same time but ultimately a moral decision often has to be made and we are back to the question of who or what makes this decision and on what basis.

The two bases that could apply are either a random selection or a guided selection basis. A random selection basis suggests that the next time the same question arises, a different moral answer might be favoured by the individual. This then raises more questions about randomly varying moral values and must lead to a chaotic state of inconsistency.

Of course, sometimes the moral values involved can be clouded and hard to sort out, but where the same question needs the same consideration, the same answer should apply and usually does. Logic, then, suggests that a guided selection takes place, but guided by whom or what?

Perhaps the answer is that the debate is really between the Intellect's experience (Ego) and the Inner Self's inherent, guiding, spiritual wisdom and that the decision will depend on which entity is more strongly registered at the time, and is additional proof of the probability of the existence of an Inner Self in each of us.

Again, given that it is a fact that many of us experience moments when we are conscious of 'other than normal' help, doesn't it seem more likely that this is due to a direct relationship with *our* spiritual Inner Self? That by being made aware of *our* specific needs and our personal circumstances, it has provided moral answers to *our* problems?

Is this perhaps due to an involuntary and momentary form of meditation – a type of instant spiritual 'tuning in' that provided an answer? Please keep in mind that the word spiritual is not meant to have any religious sense at all here.

Most of us have experienced a situation where after a night's sleep we have suddenly arrived at an answer to a troubling problem. Doesn't this suggest that something has been at work while we slept? Some additional factor has been brought into effect which has helped to provide the answer. What do you think this factor is? As this can only be due to your own mental activities, perhaps you will agree that it could be your Inner Self in action.

Renewal

Finally, all of us have had moments when we are just tired of the everyday battles and need to 'get away from it all'. Not the physical battle – this can be overcome to a large degree by a few days of rest – it's the mental battle that can be so wearying. At these times, we are unconsciously seeking some sort of mental 'time-out' to refocus ourselves or to take a breath, if you like, to enable us to go forward once again.

I suggest that all of these points are everyone's evidence that they have an Inner Self – if you like, a self-generating reservoir of spiritual support that is always there, especially when it is allowed to come to the surface, for instance during a 'time-out' period. It has been described as 'the still, small voice' within.

It will be evident from all that has been said that no one standard of belief satisfies everyone and why should it? It's a deeply personal matter that everybody has to sort out for themselves. It isn't something that others can tell you about with any acceptable degree of authority, but once you are aware of the possibility of its existence, it does require a decision from each of us about ourselves.

You may like to think about it, keeping in mind that this view is quite compatible with most religious views – it's just expressed here in non-religious terms.

The Nuts and Bolts of it all...

So, how does all of this work? Well, it might make it easier if it was assumed that the Intellect contains the bodily equivalent of a computer that is continually accepting information from all parts of the body about its condition – is it thirsty or hungry, is it in danger, is it too hot or cold, etc.? – on an instantaneous basis. This is presented to the reasoning part of the Intellect for a decision on the appropriate action to take. This is an automatic process and is a continual report on the body's physical safety or needs.

God – a balance of probabilities?

The Inner Self also provides input on a continuing basis, but unless the Intellect (Ego) is schooled to take note of this input, bodily needs often tend to shout louder and the spiritual voice is swamped out as not requiring immediate attention.

This is a part of the body's physical survival techniques, developed by evolutionary forces over many thousands of years, and often a conscious effort has to be made by the Intellect to listen to the spiritual voice and take its input into account.

How often have you said, or heard others say, 'someone up there was sure looking after me', or 'my guardian angel was looking out for me', when describing an inexplicable impulse action that turned out to be very beneficial. The 'guardian angel' concept is considered by some to be somebody who has already moved into spirit form who cares about them and is able to exercise an appropriate influence.

But perhaps it would have been closer to the truth, and more logical anyway, to have said that 'someone in there' – that is your Inner Self – was looking after you and on that occasion, being aware of your personal problem and circumstances at the time, managed to 'shout' loud enough to override your Conscious Self (Ego), to influence it to take the action that was taken.

Who would be in a better position to help fix your particular problem than your own Inner Self with its direct access to your Intellect/body and its needs? In effect, there was a problem of some magnitude which was troubling you, and when the answer was provided 'out of the blue' as it were, its value was recognised and acted upon.

It is worth noting again that this happens to all sorts of people in all sorts of situations and at all sorts of times, that is, it's not restricted to any particular person, religious beliefs, or time or situation, but fills a need when it's most needed by the individual and appears almost without effort or recognition.

However, it's the individual's choice, then, whether the advice offered is accepted or not and, to take this a bit further, it should be noted that the Intellect (Ego) may filter the message according to its educational and life biases. The appropriate action may not always be taken or may only be taken on a modified basis, so allowance for variations has to be made.

If, at that time, the body's physical needs are under stress, and safety, for example, was considered paramount, then spiritual messages may be off-loaded, as it were, until the Intellect considers that the body's safety needs are satisfied and that other items can then be downloaded and considered. But, of course, if the spiritual message was not strongly registered, then it may be lost in the process of being temporarily off-loaded. The mental computer didn't save it and other more mundane messages or thoughts took over.

When you think about this aspect a bit more, you may be aware of instances in your own life where you have not really followed through thoroughly, for no particular reason, and later wished that you had given a particular course of action more thought.

So, to get back to the main point – there is a conscious intelligent Self, the Intellect or Ego, that takes care of all matters relating to the wellbeing or proper functioning of the body, such as hunger, thirst, self-preservation, the creative functions and all other logical functions associated with normal living in today's world. Separately, there is an Inner Self – the spiritual entity of the individual that offers other advice as necessary. These two entities exist side by side, but although they co-operate on occasion, are quite separate in function.

Of course, you could simply dismiss all of this by saying that having made a successful decision, you were just lucky and leave it at that. I suppose that's one way of looking at it, but isn't this just a way of sidestepping something you don't really want to face, that is, the notion that maybe you should be giving more thought to the spiritual side of your being?

Keeping in mind that an acceptance of the concept of having an Inner Self doesn't require any specific religious beliefs, perhaps you will agree that a personal rethink is justified.

Decisions

So, let's restate what is being considered. You are being asked to accept the concept of having an 'Inner Self' or Soul, based on your own experiences and the comments made above. Another person's experiences won't help; you have to arrive at the conclusion that it is reasonable for you to accept that this is so, and then, hopefully, to continue to base your further thinking on this belief as you proceed through life.

Remember: this is a private matter and lip service won't do because *you* know if you are being sincere about it or not. This is the sort of issue which really can't be avoided by an 'I don't know' comment and left at that. It does require you to think about it and come to some decision, because your acknowledgment and acceptance of this concept is important in making progress. Personal decisions and commitment are needed as a first step.

Nobody can give you unconditional proof that an Inner Self or Soul does or doesn't exist, because to do so would be to offer physical proof of either your own or another's spiritual entity and this doesn't seem to be available.

Measurements of mental activity can be offered but sorting this out to show a confirmable spiritual component so far isn't possible. However, all of us know of individuals who are held in high esteem as leaders of society, who do exhibit high moral and spiritual values, suggesting that these factors do exist.

Certainly, Science can't help, but reasoning and being aware of the possibility of its interaction with our conscious selves on particular occasions, means that all of us have a vague and maybe uncomfortable suspicion of its existence, even though we can't see it, or prove it empirically.

This is the difficulty in trying to describe or explain a personal non-physical entity of this type to others and is a part of the confrontational process referred to earlier. A decision on the Inner Self concept is really important if you are to continue to sort out your thoughts as we are doing. Of course, you can leave it unanswered if you wish, but it will remain an incomplete and nagging part of your life.

Spiritual Barrier

To continue, it seems there is a barrier in place between these two entities – the Inner Self and the Conscious Self or Ego, probably for the following reasons:

1. To prevent the Inner Self from overloading the Conscious Self or Intellect with information that for educational or intelligence level reasons it can't handle. But, this information is always available on an 'as required' basis to those who are seeking assistance, either consciously or unconsciously.

2. To ensure that the Inner Self is unaffected by being a part of the human condition and that the mental effects of any wrongs committed on Earth are left behind when the human phase is complete.

3. To enable the Inner Self to withdraw, with the Life Force and the Conscious Self, at an appropriate time, in the event of the body's physical death.

This barrier can be overcome, first – by showing that we are aware that the barrier is there and by consciously reaching out to try to break it down through the use of meditation, and second – by having in mind that we have the wit and intelligence to understand any answers being provided and that trivial attempts at such a contact should be avoided.

Religious Influence

To suggest that some religions might have the power to bestow a particular status on the Soul, by recognising it in some way, also raises the question about whether there are differences between the status that each religion might offer.

For example, is one status better than the other just because they are acknowledged by what somebody arbitrarily decides is the true religion? Who decides this and on what basis? What does God think about this?

Some religions have claimed that Man was created in God's image and that he should, therefore, conform to their spiritual version of God. This claim ignores the fact that as their spiritual views are man-made, they can have no better idea of God's spiritual appearance than anyone else. It is their version and that's fine for them, but it doesn't advance the discussion. What is really meant by this comment is that if Mankind was created in God's image, then Man must be a spiritual being, as we are discussing here, and perhaps, you may agree, this supports the illusion of physicality, referred to earlier.

Another point to consider is this – if the Inner Self or Soul is already of God and is therefore indestructible, how can any earthly physical influence alter this? While the discipline of a religious belief may be helpful in learning to contact the Inner Self, this is not essential and might, in fact, cause problems because of other competing and confusing man-made rules peculiar to that religion.

Physically, each of us is born and dies as a *single entity* – that is, it is an inherent and personally intimate process and while it is understood that many of us dislike the thought of being alone at these times, whether we like it or not this is the condition of entry and departure from this world, regardless of what is achieved in between.

We should recognise that the fear of being alone is a fear of the unknown, and is the other side of the 'comfort coin' achieved by being part of the human race. However, as a spiritual being, this fear will no longer apply as, in my view, we will be in company of other spiritual beings after death.

Our association with, and attachment to, other humans, then, is only of importance in that it helps us to realise our spiritual and physical responsibilities here on Earth. This adds additional emphasis to the need to care for each other, in the fullest sense, while we can.

Indeed, Man is an entity consisting of three parts: 1) a physical form, 2) an intellectual entity, and 3) a spiritual entity.

Spiritual World

This is also discussed in later chapters, but perhaps should be mentioned here. It is probably fair to say that religious authorities have always claimed that the spiritual realm is a part of their exclusive sphere of knowledge and influence. Outsiders were discouraged from taking an independent interest in it by having their findings labelled as unofficial, heretical, unreliable and/or maybe even superstitious nonsense.

As has already been pointed out, it is difficult to produce evidence that everyone will accept as proof that a spiritual world exists, but most will accept the religious view that the individual possesses a Soul as correct.

May I say that if this view is held – *despite the fact that this is also scientifically unproven* – then isn't it also fair to say that having a spiritual Inner Self, called the Soul, implies that a spiritual world exists?

Science tells us that everything in the universe is based on energy, and suggests that perhaps there could be a multiplicity of different universes in existence in the same space, at the same time. So, it seems to be a small step to take to also suggest that this could include a spiritual energy world or realm that operates under the rules of 'Spiritual Physics'. As it is spiritual in nature, it wouldn't take up any space and could, therefore, co-exist unseen or unfelt right here and now on physical Earth.

Now, supposing such a spiritual barrier was breached by a person of special abilities. This person could work wondrous cures and perform feats that would apparently defy our known laws of physics because of a greater understanding of a more advanced set of laws of physics of a different world.

Could this be a reasonable explanation for the appearance and activities of Jesus, and those of the Prophets and various other holy individuals?

I know this might be a bit confrontational but try to consider this in a non-religious way. Perhaps they were spiritual visitors from another world or universe, trying to explain their special abilities for our benefit but having to speak in terms and language that could be readily understood by their largely uneducated audiences at that time. This may be a part of God's plan for Mankind's development.

After all, religions were invented by men, after a particular event or series of events had occurred, to perpetuate their version and understanding of what they felt was a spiritual experience or happening. They also tried to explain these happenings, and what *they* felt it all meant, to others.

In thinking along these lines, please remember this reasonable explanation doesn't reduce the value or meaning of the teachings of Jesus, the prophets, Mohammed, or Buddha in any way, and as God created the universe, we are all 'children' of God.

So, if it is acceptable, even if only for argument's sake, that spiritual entities are a reality of life here on Earth, the next question might relate to where these entities might live or have their existence. They would exist in their own energy plane – anywhere and everywhere. It may well be that right at this minute each of us is surrounded by spiritual energy entities going about their business, as it were, each world unknown to the other, except in special circumstances or on occasions when, perhaps, some kind of contact is enabled.

If an 'unseen energy world' seems a doubtful statement to make, just think of the Earth's magnetic energy field and radio and TV energy transmission fields, to cite some obvious and indisputable examples of unseen energy worlds. These occupy no physical space and can't be seen or felt, but are everywhere around us and we would be unaware of them except for suitable receivers and measuring devices.

So why shouldn't similar spiritual energy waveforms also surround us, waiting for us to develop the ability to 'tune in' or break through the barrier? Not believable? Why? Surely, it has to be considered a possibility.

CHAPTER FIVE

Healing

In starting a discussion on healing, it might be appropriate to describe what is meant by being unwell or having a disease. This is the same as saying that the body is uneasy about itself – that it is in a state of bodily unbalance – its functions aren't working or reacting normally for some reason. This might be due to a number of factors, such as poor nutrition or a lack of exercise, an infection of some sort, or a combination of a number of problems that add up to a feeling that we recognise as being unwell.

The Intellect is registering a disharmony – that something is not as it should be and those who have developed the ability to 'listen' to their bodies will be aware of this feeling and will probably be able to assist in its recovery more easily. Now, depending on the severity or the nature of the problem, either the body's inbuilt Repair Department –the Immune System - will take care of it with little or no additional treatment, or if, of a more serious nature, then medical advice will probably be required to assist the healing process.

Of course, there are a number of ways of approaching the healing process – all of which have their particular benefits – and it is the individual's choice of how this is to be handled. But regardless of the method chosen, you should keep your doctor informed of your actions.

While wellness is a normal body condition, it can be affected by the way in which we think about ourselves. If we adopt a depressing mental approach to life, then the result may well be that bodily functions will also be depressed and not work as well as they should, and problems will inevitably result. It doesn't matter whether the cause of the stress is external or is self-induced, body health can be affected – it is a fact that we can 'think' ourselves ill.

So, it's also reasonable to accept the proposition that we can just as easily 'think' ourselves well, and suggests that we should adopt a more realistic and open approach on how the healing process can be assisted or achieved. As choices have to be made, let's first look at the body's inbuilt physical healing abilities.

The Immune System

It seems that as a part of its survival techniques, the body is able to physically repair itself to a degree not yet fully appreciated or utilised, and it should be kept in mind that while the introduction of drugs of various sorts may provide assistance to the healing process, it is the body that is actually carrying out this activity. The drugs just make it easier.

Under normal conditions, any repairs required are automatically carried out by the Immune System as a part of its inbuilt body servicing routine. Minor illnesses and injuries usually result in obvious symptoms such as increased temperature, pain, or some other indicator, and it's these stimuli that alert the body that it is under attack and its routine responses are immediately initiated.

But, if an illness or problem is in progress where there is no indication of its existence, then no action will be taken until this occurs and the alarm is raised. This may be at a late stage in the illness and examples of this could be a previously undiscovered tumour, or a heart problem, a stroke, a burst aneurysm suddenly becoming apparent, or the involvement in a serious accident of some sort.

There may be no pain or other symptom apparent until the problem is far advanced and a breakdown occurs, triggering the body's normal repair program into action. This may be inadequate and, at this time, medical assistance may be able to bring the problem under control to allow the body to continue with its curative activity, but if time does not allow this to happen, then death may follow. However, there are instances where even critical cases have been saved and mind-body healing has played a major part in some of these instances.

Mind-Body Interaction

In discussing this aspect, keep in mind that the expenditure of physical energy is controllable by mental energy – that is, apart from an automatic body reflex response, the choice of whether physical energy is to be expended or not is the result of a prior mental energy decision.

In essence, and at a very basic level, it is being proposed that purposeful mental energy can be used to control physical energy – as the Immune System already does indirectly – and in discussing this part of our journey, it should again be noted that any general descriptions used here are those of a layman and may be open to strict correction by more expert readers in the context of their speciality.

However, you are asked to accept the meanings intended, rather than whether it is a strictly correct scientific description or not, as any obvious differences should be of a minor nature and won't alter the sense of what we are discussing, or of any conclusions offered.

As the body is controlled progressively through its life span by inbuilt switches activated by genes, hormones or proteins that come into play at various times throughout our lives, it is reasonable to consider that these switches might be controllable in some way, apart from the use of drugs.

Obvious examples of these switches are the onset of puberty during early teenage years, and perhaps later on in life its reversal, causing the decline of various abilities perceived as no longer necessary as we age.

The latter may well be an example where the logical part of the brain, during its normal body check-up, reacts to the body's reduced physical needs and condition over a period of time and assumes that this is the new norm, and automatically switches a particular function, such as a specific gene, off or on, as it is no longer necessary to the body's present functioning level.

Alteration to this condition, then, may require special intervention of some sort, such as improving an organ's physical condition through, for example, diet, exercise, or in an emergency, using drugs or some other means to correct the switching off/on action.

This is what is being proposed by mind-body healing – we are trying to use the individual's own mental energy to alter processes at a basic cellular energy level to achieve an improvement in the body's health. So, how might this be achieved?

Well, as this can only be done with the aid and co-operation of your Inner Self and the only contact at this level is by a form of meditation, it seems logical to use this approach. It is noteworthy that for many years, some individuals have achieved health improvement by their own meditative activities, but Science wouldn't accept it because the cause wasn't able to be proven. But now Science can also achieve this at a cellular level, perhaps the prospect of mind-body healing via meditation may become more acceptable.

Meditation

The process of meditation is a part of the discovery of the ultimate truth about your being – you are facing up to who you really are at a very basic level and your success, or not, will probably depend largely on your acceptance of this. This might seem a little confronting, so it is suggested that, initially, you simply acknowledge this as a background fact and, as suggested earlier, allow the meditative process to grow at a rate acceptable to yourself.

Perhaps it might be helpful to consider various questions, such as the following. When we meditate – with whom, or what, are we trying to make contact? From where do the undoubted benefits of meditation come? What is that something and what causes it to act? It has to be agreed that it is not a physical entity – it's a mental 'within' thing that has access to your mind to cause natural body reactions. It is very reasonable then, to again suggest that the answers point toward the existence of an Inner Self. Now this can be reasoned out if you wish, or initially, it can be based on an instinctive acceptance that it is so.

It is understood that this may be an unfamiliar concept and a bit confronting, but it must be obvious that if you are setting yourself up to use a treatment regime that depends on mental contact with your Inner Self, and your very practical everyday mind rejects the possibility of its existence, then you've got a conflict of interests which will probably undermine your efforts.

It is important, then, that you give strong consideration to what you are intending to achieve and, at the very least, adopt an open mind about it all. A starting point will be to accept that it is possible that an Inner Self does exist and that you might be able to effect some health improvements by your efforts. From here you should continue to go through the motions on this basis.

It might take time for observable progress to be made, and this will vary from person to person – some will have to try harder or longer than others and it will also depend on the severity of the illness. We are all individuals with different levels of acceptance, reactions and concerns.

As a race we are preconditioned to accept our physical abilities, but aren't taught to trust our minds relative to our mental energy abilities, and so we don't push the mental envelope. This also preconditions us to NOT expect the results we need, and so when it doesn't happen in the time WE THINK is sufficient for action to have taken place, then it's proof that it doesn't work, 'there you are – I told you so – it's a load of rubbish'.

Maybe the approach should be to see why it hasn't happened. Perhaps we have private reservations about the possibility of success and while this is understandable, maybe this is where the problem lies – the lack of a belief factor. It may also require time, so it goes back to the individual's perseverance.

It is understood that this process will not be accepted as a valid approach by everyone, but as there is no one standard of belief that satisfies everyone, each person has to sort this out for themselves.

It isn't something that others can tell you about with any degree of authority because it requires the person involved to reason it out for himself – that this approach is the right course of action for him to take, and then to act on this belief to the best of his ability. There can be no guarantees – only possibilities that can become probabilities.

Background Basics

But it might be helpful to gain an understanding of what contact means at a cellular level. As pointed out earlier, everything in the universe is composed of energy in one form or another. Einstein confirms this in his theory, E (energy) = M (mass) x C^2 (speed of light squared), which means that, in general terms and under some circumstances, Mass or the physical component of ALL substances can be equated to a quantity of Energy.

We are very familiar with the physical aspect of our existence on Earth, but may not be familiar with the fact that Einstein's theory is really saying that the mass of the Earth and all it contains, including ourselves, can be viewed as quantities of energy.

This is discussed more fully later, but for now an easy and obvious example that you will be familiar with would be to consider that, as about 70% of the human body's mass consists of water, then this 70% of the body's content can be expressed in energy terms as so much H_2O (2 atoms of Hydrogen and 1 atom of Oxygen). Similarly, other parts of the body – bone structure (calcium), fats, metals and salts etc. – can all be described in energy terms, and like all other matter on Earth, we are subject to the same basic laws of physics.

Keep in mind that this energy concept view not only includes the millions of cells of which our bodies are made, but also the energy generated and used by our minds to send signals to our body parts and to create our thinking processes in our everyday living activities. Without doubt, we are energy beings in an apparent physical form, using energy in all of our activities.

So, in essence, when discussing mind-body healing, meditation, we are suggesting that we can use our thinking energy in conjunction with the energy of our Inner Self to alter or affect body energy at a cellular level to achieve a physical healing result. Mind over matter.

God – a balance of probabilities?

If this seems fanciful then consider the following. Your Intellect creates mental energy when thoughts are created to carry out some task. When your Intellect directs the body to take some action it uses mental energy to do this and your body then uses energy to carry out the task. An obvious example is when the body needs refuelling – it sends an energy signal to the Intellect that it is hungry or thirsty and the appropriate physical energy action is activated to relieve this. Another example is taking evasive action when in danger, and so on.

This simply means that we are energy-based beings and everything we do relates to the use of energy, so why shouldn't our mental energies be able to take charge and influence the health of our energy bodies? Nanotechnology – the study of materials at a sub-atomic level – is now achieving results at a body cellular level and can turn processes off and on by altering energy content at this level.

However, it's very understandable to have doubts about all of this, because our mental conditioning over the years has emphasised the physical approach to healing and has tended to ignore that a mental approach can also be relevant. Remember the earlier comments about 'miracle healing' and how this has been ridiculed over the years? Maybe this should be looked at afresh.

By accepting that you can think yourself well, and by providing the opportunity to achieve this, you will gain confidence and provide the best environment for an improvement in your situation to take place. Remember that this is not an instant gratification exercise and in the same way that improvement with drugs etc. often takes time, so the mental approach has to be given time to work. But, it should also be said that speedy results have also been documented, on occasion.

But ask your doctor about the possibility of controlling or eliminating diseases by other than medical means and he will probably be a bit dismissive, and eventually just suggest that it's an unscientific approach, which is unproven and a bit fanciful. What is really meant is that because the medical profession can't provide a scientific explanation for these occurrences when they do happen, then, in their view, either the original diagnosis was incomplete, or it's regarded as a 'remission' without a cause. A case of preferring a non-explanation to an unorthodox explanation.

Existing Medication

If a mind-body form of healing, such as meditation is being considered, it should be clearly understood that it is **not** being suggested here that existing medical treatment of any disease should be altered or discontinued in any way.

Any and all treatment of a disease that aids in the healing process is most acceptable, and with this in mind, it is better that all forms of treatment should become a part of the overall regime in consultation with your doctor. After all, it really doesn't matter what fixes the problem, the important aspect is that healing does take place, with due acknowledgement of what caused it.

Of course, time must be allowed for these reactions to occur and this will vary according to the type of problem, the individual's age, health and mental condition and so on. On some occasions, the time factor may be fairly short, but on others, a longer time might be necessary, so a slower reaction should not be taken as evidence that nothing is being achieved.

Organ Renewal

It is undeniable that there are cell renewal processes going on all the time within the body. An easy example to illustrate this is that every few months a new layer of skin cells is created, from within the body, to take the place of skin cells on the surface which are either degraded by the sun, or worn out by normal physical activity. Doesn't this mean that from a skin point of view you are automatically being renewed every so many months, without you being aware of it? Where do those cells come from and what causes them to be made? Yes, I know it's a natural renewal process – but isn't this just saying that it is possible to renew parts of ourselves if we only knew how. In the case of the skin, it's an automatic process – why isn't it also automatic for other requirements?

Consider finger and toe nails as another obvious example. These are growing constantly, the new cells being formed to replace the dead cells which are cut off or worn down. This process is also taking place with other organs at different rates so that the organs you were born with no longer exist, having been replaced many times over, according to need.

Doesn't all of this suggest that the body is able to remake itself according to each person's existing DNA blueprint, and that a part of its normal functioning is to carry this out for selected parts of the body at defined rates and times? In other words, this remarkable natural ability is there if only we could learn to control it to our greater advantage.

Let's take this a bit further. Science tells us that our bodies are constructed according to a blueprint laid down by the individual's DNA, and at conception, before birth, cells are created and directed to proceed to an appointed place in the developing body to carry out the construction of particular organs. These organs will perform specialised tasks for their lifetime. Later, as these cells age, replacement cells will be required to enable the organs to continue to function and these are provided as pre-programmed basic cell units from, for example, the bone marrow, for use on an *as required* basis.

This process of the provision of new cells then continues all through our lives as part of the body's normal automatic repair program. But, supposing the new cells used for the division are in some way faulty, then perhaps these will provide faulty cells that may become uncontrolled and a cancer, or an unusual growth pattern, becomes apparent. It is incidental whether the faulty cell might have been caused by some avoidable action – smoking or excessive sun tanning comes to mind – or if it is naturally and unavoidably self-generated in some inherent way.

Think of the millions of cells which go to make up the human body and are being replaced periodically; it's a wonder that errors of this type don't occur more often. Perhaps they do and in most cases are eliminated by the body's Immune System, and we only become aware of those that are more virulent, or are escapees, that emerge later to cause problems such as tumours or a cancer of some sort.

God – a balance of probabilities?

If we are all recycling and renewing ourselves as we go through life, using our individual DNA blueprint to do this, the next question has to be why shouldn't we be able to reconstruct healthy replacement body parts as needed? In the case of the liver we can already do this. If a part of your liver is removed, it can grow back to a normal functioning capability, of its own accord, reasonably soon afterwards.

I know the concept of self-renewal may sound pretty far fetched, but if we have the ability to replace specialised cells on an automatic basis and still have the original blueprint to work from, why can't we extend this process further? Can you imagine, say, entering into a retreat of some sort and by a process of intense meditation over some months, causing the construction of, say, part of a new heart muscle or lung tissue, or whatever, to replace an existing diseased part? No? Why not?

You will be aware, from general knowledge, that there are examples of flesh renewal during the normal wound healing processes, of new bone cells growing to fill a gap between broken bones and also of nerve endings growing towards each other to replace a missing bit. Aren't these simple examples of what we are talking about? It seems to be a small further step to take, to try to take charge of this natural process and purposely try to grow new bits and pieces within the body, using the body's own resources.

It can already be done outside the body, and in recent years, reports from the Royal Melbourne Hospital, indicate that a successful cultivated stem cell implant trial has already caused successful bone regrowth in a specially selected number of bedridden patients where, critically, this has not been possible by other means to date. Other successful trials have included the 'relining' of arthritis ridden joints.

Heart muscle cell implants are also growing successfully and working in conjunction with existing patient heart muscle cells. The successful completion of these trials will herald a new era in healing and it seems likely that rejection problems may soon be overcome.

The practice of meditation is independent of, but can be supplementary to, most religious teachings. It is practised by many Christian, Jewish, Islamic and other Eastern traditions and while this process can be carried out by anyone, you may find it advantageous to first get a good grounding in meditation with the assistance of a suitably experienced practitioner. But keep in mind that you need to know the basics of meditation, not vague Eastern religious beliefs, so seek out independent professional teachers in this field.

If you like, meditation can be described as a form of prayer, directed to your spiritual core, or Inner Self, and you may find this more acceptable if you consider that your spiritual Inner Self is really God's local 'on-site agent'.

Finally, the fact that you are able to get in touch with your Inner Self in this way is not only evidence that we can reprogram our thinking to eliminate or modify the state of a disease, it is also confirmation that you have a Spiritual Self within and, therefore, that a spiritual world exists. It also confirms for me, that God, the Supreme Spirit, exists.

Death – An Introduction to a New Life?

So, what is the difference between a live person and a dead person, physically? There's no difference – at that point the body is still the same as before in terms of its physicality and the value of its parts is unaltered. The difference is that its gift of life energy has been withdrawn and is no longer available for it to function. A bit like an electrical motor – when you withdraw its energy by switching off the power supply, it can no longer function either – at that point, its value too is the sum of its parts in the marketplace.

The true value of each is in what it can accomplish when switched on, and when this is negated then its intrinsic value is whatever its parts are worth, for whatever purpose, from then on.

However, it is an inescapable fact that Man is marching toward his death from the time he is born, but if the concept of an indestructible Spiritual Self is accepted in the same way that we accept that the physical Self is temporary, it becomes a normal process of living. It could be said that death is not so much the taking of life, but the release of life from the restrictions that the physical body has placed on it.

So, a discussion about death and dying really requires that the individual has to face up to a decision about his beliefs about the existence or not of a personal Inner Self or Soul, for it to mean something. If this concept is not accepted then much of what follows will also be unacceptable because inevitably it relates to the progress of the Inner Self. But see what you think about it all after you've read it.

When you think about this aspect a little you will realise that life itself is full of uncertainties that Man strives to overcome, and each advancement in knowledge brings both advantages and dangers. It is his ability to make use of these advantages and avoid the dangers that largely determines how long he will live.

Death, then, is the only certainty in our physical lives and in other parts of this work reference has been made to the competition for attention, within our minds, between the physical and spiritual entities of our existence. Death is the final arbiter of this competition.

Physical death can be put off for just so long. That is, the body has an inbuilt use-by date, which may be shortened by some inadvertent action, or able to be extended for a limited period, but as the spiritual entity is thereby released for other duties, death is just a signal that the existing physical body is no longer suitable for that spirit's needs.

We have no certain prior knowledge of what lies ahead when death occurs, but perhaps some of the fears involved can be minimised. The physical body dies when its automatic life support systems fail for whatever reason, and because it can no longer carry out its prime function of providing support to the Life Force within, the body is no longer of interest from a spiritual point of view. It has served its purpose.

Of course, the physical body is still important to others in a close relationship, because it is the outward representation of the Life Force energy, that is, the individual's intelligent Self plus the Inner Self that was the real reason for the relationship in the first place. With the body's death comes the sad realisation of the closing down of that physical relationship, but perhaps the opening up of a closer spiritual nearness.

Natural death cannot be avoided and it may well be that this is a signal that there is little advantage in proceeding in that particular physical form, because of a particular weakness and/or because the spirit is ready to advance to a new type of life form. It may also help those who remain to understand that their tenure on life is also temporary and may provide an opportunity for them to reconsider their own lives.

The process of dying may be physically uncomfortable because of the body's strong inbuilt survival instincts, but this depends on circumstances and an acceptance of the inevitable. Keep in mind that the fear of death is part of the inherent survival instinct, referred to earlier, that was embellished and used by priests as a part of their means of controlling the population.

This was done by the introduction of two doctrines. First, the frightening concept of a personal God who would exact judgment after death, for real or imagined wrongs (sins) on Earth, and second, the concept of heaven and hell as a reward or punishment.

So, stop right here and now, and think for a moment what terrible sins you have been guilty of during your lifetime. Probably, when you were fairly young you disobeyed your parents, maybe pinched a sweet or something similar from a shop somewhere, perhaps cheated at something, told a few lies, broke a window or two, were involved in a few minor scrapes. Nothing earth-shattering yet, so I don't think God would be very interested, would he?

When you became an adult you probably still indulged in a few untruths and maybe got in and out of a few more adult scrapes here and there, maybe let a few people down, but generally you lived according to the laws of the land and gradually made your way in the world. This is a part of our general education about living within a society.

Still nothing of any great consequence so that, by and large, you became a part of society in which the 'do unto others as you would have them do unto you' rule seemed fairly sensible, because it gave everyone a fair go and provided us all with a measure of mutual self-protection for ourselves and our families.

Doesn't all of this suggest to you that you are pretty much '**a failure at sinning**' and, while I am not suggesting that you should lift your game here, it's certainly nothing for God to be concerned about, is it? OK, there are some exceptions, but the laws of each country provide remedies for these to institute some corrective action, so that some balance is eventually struck to try to offset this moral breakdown. This is not the place to discuss how effective this action might be but simply to establish that the 'sinner' has been brought to account here on Earth.

But regardless, the continuing survival of the Inner Self or Soul is undoubted, and if the artificial religious concepts of 'the need to be saved' and 'an impending consignment to hell' etc. are removed, it will be seen that spiritually there is little to fear from death, because it only relates to the body, not the essential Self – the real you. It's really a fear of the unknown enhanced by inherited religious beliefs.

God – a balance of probabilities?

Now, it's not the intention here to trivialise this aspect in any way, or to overlook the fact that the manner of physical death may be distressing, particularly to others. Part of any growth process is the acceptance of change and those who are overly concerned about the prospect of dying should keep in mind that, at suitable times throughout our lives, we all discarded those earthly things that were no longer useful or necessary.

You may agree that this gets down to the very heart of the difficulties experienced in dying. It is the ultimate rejection of all things physical that we have been taught to cherish all our lives, and also highlights one of the great problems we have, when we try to envisage life after death in terms of life as we know it here on Earth.

Death is really the process by which we change worlds and it may well be that the act of dying is really a shift in conscious energy awareness into that of being in a purely spiritual energy state. It is suggested that this is not a situation of anonymity and darkness that everyone fears, but an awakening into a new and different reality.

This is also discussed in comments made later about dreaming and it is suggested that this is the same state in which we will find ourselves having died – a spiritual energy form that replaces a physical energy form.

Of course, as physical beings it isn't possible to know what a spirit world is really like, but if accounts offered by those who have had a near death experience are accepted, the person who is in the process of dying is met by very caring spiritual beings. These will ease the dying process and help the new arrival to become familiar with his new existence and its requirements.

These are likely to have the appearance of a bright light, or may temporarily take a variety of forms depending on the person's beliefs, traditions and culture. This 'bright light' concept is not inconsistent with the view that spiritual beings are made up of a type of energy, because a bright light is simply energy made visible in the Intellect's 'eye'.

However, whilst all of this is pure conjecture until we find out for ourselves, it is in line with the whole process of spiritual development, suggested earlier, as the reason for our existence.

But let's try to make this discussion a bit more relevant by placing it in more present day terms. Most of us grow up with the general understanding that our stay on Earth is temporary – that after an indeterminate period of some years, during which we develop our personal skills, abilities, and relationships, we will die as physical beings. As our physical bodies are only of importance while on Earth, then you may also agree that their location at the time of death is really unimportant, and any memorial, wherever located, will continue to serve to provide a mental focus point for those remaining.

Now suppose that instead of concentrating on the alleged awfulness of a physical death (and it should be kept in mind that it may not be so for the individual involved), we substitute it with the concept that the dying process allows us to be spiritually promoted to another life in a new sphere of activity.

God – a balance of probabilities?

Of course, as a spiritual world occupies no physical space and has no need for any physical conditions of existence, its location could be anywhere. Part of the deal would be the certain knowledge that any introduction to this new position would only be after a suitable briefing period had taken place, and that we would be suitably equipped with senses to handle whatever came along.

A spirit world would not require that we need any of the physical attributes – eyes, ears, legs, arms etc. that we rely on now for our daily physical activities. But keep in mind that as we normally process the results of these activities mentally and can still experience them when dreaming, there is no reason why this same mental processing shouldn't continue to be a part of the new Spiritual (energy) Self. Fanciful? Yes. True? Who knows? It's very reasonable and well within the balance of probabilities, so now let's look at facts.

The only facts we have are:

1. That each of us would be able to confirm that it is true and quite normal for people to have died during our lifetimes, and that there is no certain knowledge where the Life Force, the personality, of these people has gone, only that it is absent and they are no longer available to us.

2. That you and I are aware that all of us have an unknown lifespan and may also die at any time. Death then is the only certainty in life, there are no other facts.

Now, take this a bit further and use a balance of probabilities approach in the absence of any other measure. Isn't it reasonable to say, because of your general understanding about your stay on Earth, that the natural progression of a child learning to be an adult, gaining mental and spiritual development through the process of living, raising a family and so on, would be pointless if there is nothing further after physical death?

Is there any reason you can think of, not just a fear but a reasoned opinion, which would suggest that the physical process of dying is not just a *normal natural progression* which might lead to another existence? For example, it could be as a transition to another form of life appropriate for whatever lies ahead – maybe a spiritual existence, but not necessarily of a religious kind.

Keep in mind that there is no factual evidence of the existence of any spiritual version of heaven or hell. Keep in mind too, that **other than death there are no other facts**, despite what various religions may claim.

So you have a choice between adopting an optimistic or a pessimistic view, and as you can't alter this situation and there is no reason why you should accept a pessimistic view, why not accept an optimistic view in line with the *normal* earthly progression referred to above. It has to be agreed that this progression is an earthly fact – why not also in the afterlife?

However, there is a reason why some indecision is a part of our normal approach to this subject. If there was no doubt about the 'hereafter' then mass suicides might be encouraged by those who thought that they could easily improve their lot by so doing. In my view this would be a tragic contradiction of the reason for Mankind's existence and, therefore, some continuing doubt is a healthy sign.

A very current example of this is to consider the distorted Islamic view whereby Paradise is achieved by self-destruction in the process of killing 'unbelievers'. They go to their death willingly to gain the benefit of an 'afterlife', regardless of the fact that, apart from committing an inherent and unnatural act of killing others to achieve this, they are purposely and artificially interrupting the natural flow of their own life cycle.

However, it should be emphasised that it is not being suggested here that you shouldn't regret, or not be grieved about, the loss of a particular person's physical presence, but simply to point out that the transition that occurs is probably not to be feared any more than any other *normal natural process* such as birth. That both processes can be physically demanding, as has been said in other parts of this essay, is not in any way denied or minimised, but it is quite a normal process and as such, well within our capabilities.

Supposing you had the task of contriving the continuing birth, development and death of a species on Earth, given that it involves spiritual and physical entities, could you come up with a better and a more straightforward process than now exists?

Finally, if you feel that the spiritual component of Mankind doesn't exist, or also dies at physical death, then there isn't any point in you being concerned about anything to do with an afterlife, is there? You are going to die and that's that – finish!

But, a deeper reflection on our individual life experiences will show that this viewpoint is negativism to the extreme and is quite out of balance with the basic reasons why we are here.

Regardless of whether you hold religious beliefs or not, physical death is unavoidable and none of us will really know what is entailed until it happens, but as a 'balance of probabilities' approach suggests otherwise, a 'finish' viewpoint ought be rejected as untenable because, in my view, the end is really the beginning of a new existence.

Grieving

We've been discussing death and beyond from a spiritual aspect, pointing out the probability that this is a transition to another form of life, but we shouldn't ignore the effect that the death or loss of somebody might have on the lives of those remaining. They have to make adjustments to their lives here on Earth that will be most difficult, particularly in the initial stages.

Of course, it must be understood that these types of problems should really be discussed with those better qualified to provide answers and, no doubt, there are many excellent books written by these professionals which will be of benefit.

But as grieving can also be part of our general discussion, it is hoped that the following will be considered just good common sense and helpful, in some small way, in trying to come to grips with what has happened.

God – a balance of probabilities?

Earlier, mention was made of the special 'I' person that we are all aware of in relationship to our Inner Selves, and the various personas that we have to adopt in our public lives. A few comments might be appropriate in the context of these subjects.

1. It is very reasonable for the remaining person to be upset by the death of a partner or relative because a major part of their lives has been disrupted, and it is often difficult to know where to start in picking up the pieces to continue normal living. So remember to be kind to yourself at this time – give yourself permission to grieve in the way and at the time that suits you best, regardless of what others may think you should do.

   It is beneficial to develop the art of listening to what your body/mind is telling you. Include others as you wish, but it is your choice – be guided by how you feel and if you wish to sit quietly listening to music or reading a book, then you should do just that. If you want to take part in some other activity then, again, do just that, regardless of what others think is best for you.

   It's also a mixed up time, but it's very normal for you to be sad at the loss and to be happy at the memories you have. This is a part of the healing process but remember that you should also find time to prepare yourself to be involved with others, perhaps after a few weeks.

2. Remember you are *still the same person you were*, but some of your public persona has changed. For example, you may have been a parent, a husband or a wife, a home and family manager, and where a small family business exists,

a business confidante/advisor/assistant, on top of any other skills you were trained for earlier. One or two of these names will no longer apply, but *all of those considerable skills are still there*, waiting to be used, as and when you decide to do so.

Obviously, nobody is unchanged by the loss of a partner. For a superficial example, from a woman's point of view, the title of 'Mrs William Whoever' may no longer be an apt title, but 'Joan Whoever' is still the same person as before. That is, the special 'I' person, your Inner Self – *the essential you* – is unharmed and unchanged and the real basics for living are still there.

3. On the other hand, if you wish to adopt a 'business as usual' attitude, then with the proviso that you should remember to listen to, and make allowances for, what your body/mind is telling you, that's fine too. But it's unrealistic to expect that no reaction or reduced performance will be experienced for some time. Again, be kind to yourself.

   You may feel, on reflection, that the skills you now have, and have taken for granted for years, will generate opportunities for you to build a new persona for the years ahead, so start to make plans for your future life even if these are altered as you go along. It is an acknowledgement that the present and future is more important than the past. This is not to forget the past, but simply to place it in its proper perspective, relative to living now.

4. You may find that it would be beneficial to change where you live, because of changed circumstances. At an appropriate time, perhaps after some months or when you feel more settled and able to handle this type of activity, try to assess what your new life's requirements will be. But don't move for the wrong reasons. Seek the advice of others to help in your decision, always remembering that it is *your decision* for reasons *important to you* and that the timing is for you to set.

5. Where there are painful memories, keep in mind that the past has gone and can only affect the present to the extent that you allow it. Certainly initially, look at these as often as you wish and acknowledge that they are troubling, but accept also that they can't be altered, so eventually they need to be put aside. Lock them away in a mental drawer and leave them to subside in importance. You can always rouse them when you feel like it – they'll still be available.

   When your mind wanders towards that territory, learn to recognise what's happening and, if appropriate, stop it short. Purposely divert to some other activity. You don't need to be involved, again, with anything of concern in the past – it was only of real importance at that time. The danger here is that it can lead to a 'feeling sorry for yourself' attitude that can be quite enervating and hard to shift. Why should you allow something that is now in the past to continue to upset today's living?

6. From a financial point of view, be wary of investment opportunities at this time particularly from well meaning friends. It's better to hold off until you are better able to sort these types of things out for yourself and, if you wish,

at that time seek specialised advice from reputable brokers who are usually covered by some sort of ethical guarantee.

Finally, while grieving is a very normal and natural process, its expression must not be allowed to interfere with the fact that you are still the same person as before, with your own special needs, in order for you to go on living your life. You do need to take charge of your life once more.

So, after a period, that you determine is acceptable to you, you should place your grieving to one side, and go forward once again to whatever lies ahead. Please understand there is no suggestion that you shouldn't remember the past at appropriate times, but this mustn't be allowed to interfere with your future.

PART THREE

Who Are You?

Part Three requires you to stand up and be counted – it examines spirituality, the reason why Man is here, ethical considerations, choice and chance factors and, in continuing the process of self-discovery, also highlights Man's responsibility for environmental care, Gaia. It discusses whether a 'religion' is necessary, and regardless, whether a relationship with God is a choice available to Mankind.

Robert Rowe

CHAPTER SIX

Spirituality

This chapter discusses Man's spiritual identity and offers a reason for his existence, and also questions reality. It is undeniable that Mankind has an inbuilt knowledge of his spiritual heritage that defies rationalisation, because whenever this is attempted he inevitably arrives at an inconclusive position rather than a finality. There are always loose ends which become matters of opinion.

This is simply a case of a failure of logic when applied to a state of mind that, by its very nature, is not always definable by reason or logic. It is a part of our emotional make-up that can be ignored but which ultimately surfaces or confronts us, repeatedly, for resolution.

Man has been given an inbuilt survival instinct as an aid to physical existence, and so he finds it difficult to die, even when it is obvious that he will do so. At the same time, he has always had a nagging thought that maybe there is more to life than his present physical existence shows. But this is a contradiction of everything his physical senses are telling him and is difficult to accept, perhaps because of an apparent reluctance of the physical mind to accept both spiritual and physical concepts at this stage of his development.

However, a moment's thought will show that a conscious choice between these two concepts isn't necessary or desirable. The conscious acceptance of the physical concept should lead progressively to the acceptance of the spiritual concept, in accordance with the individual's ability to reason this out. They are two different concepts of living that are irrevocably related to each other.

That natural physical death occurs at an appropriate time is undoubted and means that the eventual automatic adoption of a spiritual entity is a normal transition process. This is not necessarily more desirable, from a physical existence point of view, but ultimately unavoidable and has to be accepted, under whatever circumstances apply at the time.

Keeping in mind that the fundamental basis of the universe is energy in all its forms, the following discussion may be helpful in considering these matters.

Life Force – Definition

Reference has been made to the three types of energy existing in Mankind.

1. Living body energy needed to behave as a physical being.

2. Intelligent energy which considers alternatives and having made a decision, directs the body's actions.

3. The Inner Self or spiritual energy component.

The combination of the intelligent energy and the spiritual energy could be referred to as the Life Force because these are the basic essentials for intelligent life to exist and it is this combination which forms the basis for the ongoing entity – the Soul – to perform its new task.

Flora and fauna may exhibit the same living energy to grow and to behave with the degree of intelligence necessary for their existence as particular species on Earth, and to this extent do have a relationship with Mankind. But while there is no way of knowing whether these life forms have a knowledge of the concept of Self or not, it seems unlikely.

But it is reasonable to assume that, regardless of the nature, shape, or size of the host object, the type of living energy powering its cell functions is the same for all species, because the alternative to this is to say that there are as many types of living energies as there are types of species of life forms. This is an unnecessary complication as the difference seems to be mainly in how the living energy is arranged for each species to use.

The inherent value of the species, then, resides in the intelligent type of energy contained in the host object, rather than in the host object itself, because this enables the realisation of the possibility of the existence of an Inner Self. For example, if an animal or tree suddenly improved its intelligence level to the stage where it could be aware of an Inner Self, then its status would be altered considerably.

But, in all cases, the "host" body's main raison d'être is to survive in its world, in order to preserve the intelligent energy which occupies it and directs its activities to fulfil its life's purpose. The importance placed on this is evidenced by the intense will to live shown on some occasions, despite quite adverse conditions, and in discussing Mankind, you will be aware that there are many examples of the body's refusal to die, when logic suggests that it should do so.

These are a measure of the inbuilt support systems the body possesses and while the intelligent energy force (Intellect) cannot exist in the host body without the operational energy force to support it, the operational energy force can exist without the intelligent energy force.

The body continues to exist but without direction or consciousness, and the continuing absence of the intelligent energy force, then, is sufficient proof that the host body is no longer able to function as a part of that species, and its status is altered. An example of this could be where an unconscious person is kept alive but has no measurable conscious electrical brain activity, or other similar response, over a period of time, apart from that necessary to keep the dormant body functioning.

It should be kept in mind that the Inner Self may still be in residence, but in the absence of the intelligent energy there is no basis for contact with the body. A bit like a car motor that is idling without a driver, so the mindless body will also continue to just exist (idle) as long as basic survival conditions allow.

There are also many examples of where the body is entering into the process of dying, but inexplicably recovers. It is suggested that the Inner Self may have assumed control and, in conjunction with the Intellect, has not allowed death to happen. This might result in what is described as a near death experience.

As the living energy ceases with the death of the body, the intelligent energy and the Inner Self combine together to become the ongoing Soul in readiness for its new duties.

Man's Self-Awareness

Consciousness, or awareness of being alive, as distinct from being aware of what is necessary to sustain life, is an innate function of the Intellect, and is probably confined to Mankind as the dominant life form on Earth.

It is Man's ability to use his Intellect to become aware of his spirituality that leads to the awareness of his relationship with all other life forms and the possibility of the existence of a spiritual world, which if taken to its ultimate point is, in my opinion, confirmation of God's existence. But more of this later.

This awareness does not necessarily have or imply any religious meaning of any kind, and as evidence of a spiritual world has to be a personal experience to be fully believed and accepted, it is not possible to make any broad conclusive comment that is acceptable to all. It is possible, however, to say that there are sufficient first person experiences documented to offer a high degree of probability that a spiritual world exists. This was discussed earlier.

It is also pertinent to repeat that at some time or other during their lives, most people have been helped to arrive at a difficult decision, or take some particular course of action that was not based on logic or experience, but felt right at that time. It is suggested that this is probably guidance of a spiritual nature via the Inner Self, which was able to manifest itself on that occasion.

It may help to explain the flashes of genius that some people experience and it may be that there are those, with particular gifts, who are more tuned in to this type of guidance. That is, they are better able to overcome the contact barrier on a continuing basis than others, thus leading to outstanding performances in particular fields of activity. However, the ability to carry out 'normal' tasks is often impaired almost as a counterbalance for having this improved activity.

We consider them as geniuses, but they regard their abilities as part and parcel of their normal intellectual activity and, without denying the value of this activity, usually downplay any great personal responsibility for it; it's just there. If they are right, it is reasonable to explain their increased intellectual ability as being due to an inherent continuing assistance of the type suggested.

It will be seen, then, that while the reasoning and creative parts of the mind work together, the ready acceptance of the input from the Inner Self is quite a separate matter. This requires a disciplined effort to ensure that all parts can work together for the body's wellbeing. If, however, time is made available on a regular basis for this type of contact to occur, such as by meditation, then with practice, the same degree of effort will not be required to overcome the barrier.

Spiritual Identity

Physical bodies are generally easy to identify because of differences in physical appearance, but identical twins can cause confusion, and to avoid any doubt we are given names. But the question of an identity label of some sort being applied to the Inner Self seems to me to be quite irrelevant, as a spiritual entity will be recognised by the make-up of its energy level, which like numbers cannot be duplicated without being one and the same entity.

Spiritually, then, each of us is a separate and complete entity and will be recognisable by our individual energy content. Labels will be quite unnecessary.

If it is difficult to accept the Inner Self concept as a separate spiritual entity, then it might be helpful to point out that a denial of the existence of spiritual beings is also a denial of the existence of God. This is a conclusion that perhaps you are not really prepared to make without a great deal more thought. It seems to me that one proposition leads to another. A belief in a spiritual Self also implies a belief in a spiritual world and in the existence of God.

Looking at this slightly differently – if something exists, then originally there must have been a set of circumstances or sequence of events to create it and an intelligence of some sort to set it all going. The reverse approach is also true – a belief in God, the supreme Spirit, just has to include a spiritual world which is populated by spiritual entities, leading to the strong probability that Man has a Spiritual Self or Soul.

This does not preclude any existing theories of the evolution of the universe, but just acknowledges that in the beginning there was an intelligence we call God, from whom everything has flowed.

The alternative to this is to have no belief in anything other than what can be seen, felt and experienced as an earthly physical being, and that anything outside of these experiences is apparently imaginary, or a mental aberration of some sort. Doesn't this approach simply say that Man's emotional experiences over the centuries are of little value and can be ignored? I think this is a form of nihilism or extreme negativism.

It really depends on what sort of yardstick you want to use to measure the problem. An all- inclusive yardstick that allows for the existence of the mystery of life and all that that means, in my opinion, must lead you to the acceptance of God as the Supreme Being. A limited yardstick based on a narrow view must lead to a limited outcome and while this might be convenient as you can avoid having to come to grips with the larger problem, it's not a very satisfactory way to deal with the most important aspect of your life, is it?

It will be appreciated, then, that at this point, before going much further, it might be worthwhile taking time out to satisfy yourself about what you think about it all. It should also be said again that accepting the existence of God and a spirit world does not necessarily require, or imply, the *acceptance of any particular religion,* or the *need* to accept any particular religious beliefs or dogmas.

You can relate to God in your own way as simply as you please but, of course, this has to be on a sincere, spiritual basis. Keep in mind that this is a personal discovery that relies only on your own logic and innermost feelings. How this is decided is up to the individual, but a relationship, via your Inner Self, would seem to be the simplest and easiest method to adopt as it allows your innermost feelings to surface at times most suited to this purpose. This decision leads to an existence free of artificially induced guilt and provides a more truthful and less stressful approach to the individual's lifestyle.

Earthly Relationships

The view that Man shares a basic common life force with all living things, regardless of whether they are micro-organisms, insects, fish, birds, animals or vegetation, is a reasonable statement to make, as all of these have developed and live under common conditions, here on Earth.

The main differences between Man and these various life forms is his physical and mental evolutionary situation which allows him to be aware that he possesses an Inner Self, and has the mental capacity to consider the implications of this, as we are now doing. Apart from this, the variations in motor energy are those necessary to carry out the bodily functions required by each species.

We can all establish, through observation, that our Earth consists of two main groups – animate and inanimate things or objects. The crossover point between these may vary slightly according to the reference authority selected, but it is probably sufficient to refer to animate objects as those showing evidence of possessing Life Force, by proof of intelligence and/or size growth by cell division and/or by having the ability to move of their own volition in an ordered way.

Inanimate objects, then, don't show this evidence or have this ability, but as both animate and inanimate objects consist of the same elements in differing combinations, allowances should be made for new discoveries or definitions of life forms in the future. It also suggests that a once animate object or thing that no longer exhibits this Life Force in total, automatically has to be regarded as an inanimate object and loses its inherent value as such.

Reason for Spiritual Existence

Perhaps as a kind of lead in to these aspects we could stop for a brief minute and think about Mankind's development over the thousands of years he has existed. Man has survived all sorts of disasters and from a basic origin has gradually built up a great understanding of himself and his world. This is an inbuilt and continuing process.

He started out by making assumptions based on likelihoods or possibilities, and then sorted these out over the years until, based on new knowledge and/or experience, these assumptions have become probabilities and facts on which he could rely.

Doesn't this strongly suggest that, like our forebears, we are also a part of a grand chain of development, and wouldn't this logical process, each building on previous achievements, be a complete waste if it were all for no reason? There have been plenty of opportunities for us to destroy ourselves and our world, yet this has been avoided. So isn't it reasonable to say that based on our historical growth, our physical and mental abilities will keep growing into the future.

God – a balance of probabilities?

As our mental growth has also occurred in recognisable stages, it seems reasonable to suggest that, given the opportunity, our **spiritual** life will also grow in stages, to achieve the level of understanding required to progress further. This may also require a number of visits (reincarnations?) to Earth, or other places (?), as part of this spiritual apprenticeship.

Yes, I know this is controversial, but even though it's thinking on a different plane, it is in line with the historical developmental approach of our species, and in this context it isn't really too way-out. Why not think about it a little more and see if it doesn't make a sort of sense? If you find this a bit 'stretchy', then think of it as one of a number of possibilities.

Just as each person benefits from the sum total of the inherited Life Force development, so it is part of each person's responsibility to develop his mental abilities as much as his personal circumstances allow, to further advance Mankind.

During this time the spirit world may have the ability to, on occasion, still influence those remaining on Earth who are receptive or tuned in to its contact. Obviously, those whose mental abilities have not developed beyond the satisfaction of their basic living requirements, will add little to the further development of their Life Force, while others, being more tuned in, will have the opportunity to expand it greatly. It may well be that this continuing development also assists in determining the selection of any future Life Force activities, whatever these might be.

A view has been expressed concerning those among us who are known as savants – these are people who, for example, can carry out incredible mathematical calculations or feats of memory, but who aren't able to carry out some of the more mundane simple tasks associated with normal living, suggesting that these people are, in effect, the reverse of most of us. That is, we have difficulty carrying out the mental tasks that they find easy, and they have difficulty in doing the relatively simple physical tasks necessary for living on Earth, which we regard as easy. Perhaps, they are future identities who have accidentally slipped back into our world.

It is of interest that around the 1930s Carl Jung, a German psychologist, developed a theory of the existence of the 'collective unconscious', a source of knowledge of unknown origin that is available to all, to provide each species with the basic knowledge needed to survive in its world, according to its ability to understand and use it. I suggest that this is an explanation for a savant's abilities.

That is, they have the ability to breach the barrier, referred to earlier, automatically, or are able to 'tap' into a spiritual source of knowledge without effort – something that we have to strive to achieve. They may have already partially achieved abilities normally only available as a part of a spiritual existence, and the price paid for this might be to lose some of the basic abilities to live on Earth without assistance.

Taking this further, if we accept that as physical beings we are also developing our spiritual abilities in preparation for whatever lies ahead, perhaps the Savants are already ahead of the rest of us in their spiritual development. They might really belong to another world where their mental abilities would be considered normal and in line with the physics of that world. Our knowledge of our present physical world might be quite useless in this other, more spiritual world and we would be regarded as backward, in the same way as we regard their abilities as being advanced.

I think the reason for our existence, then, is to enable the various levels of mental and spiritual growth to be increased to a level suitable for the next stage of spirituality. Spiritual growth is a necessary part of the human evolutionary process, because without spiritual growth Mankind will stagnate and probably regress back to a more primitive state. The increasing interest in the practice of meditation and, for example, its extension into mind-body healing, may be a welcome indication of a general advancement of Man's spiritual development.

The host body is simply there to provide a suitable physical means of supporting or housing the Spiritual Self in a physical world while this development is occurring. However, it should be noted that because Man is aware of his Life Force and its spiritual relationship, and that he has the ability and responsibility to advance its progress, then any action he takes to retard its growth should be regarded as a universal moral wrong.

Where this type of degenerative activity becomes extreme, it should be considered a form of insanity – a failure of the mental abilities of the host body for whatever reason – and it is suggested that the barrier between mind and spirit effectively screens the possibility that such insane energy could proliferate in spiritual worlds.

It may well be that spiritual influence could, on some occasions, so affect those who are especially receptive that spiritual representations or ghosts are seen or felt. These may be mental images which are so vivid as to apparently impact on the individual visually and/or physically.

Perhaps at this point there should be some mention of poltergeists and similar activities in special places, and while we can speculate on the cause, there is no definitive information available. Where it is a confirmed type of activity, it may well be a function of the viewer's mind or spirit interacting with, or reacting against, a spiritual contact. This confused state is then projected outward and may affect others in the vicinity. It may, in fact, simply suggest that an unstable energy situation has been created that should immediately be discontinued.

Uncontrolled activities of any sort are disturbing and it is very natural that Man should show concern and try to make sense of it all. Given that spiritual energy is involved it should not be surprising, on occasion, that uncontrolled physical action of various sorts might take place, as energy and matter are interchangeable under some circumstances, as indicated earlier in this discussion.

The confusion and/or violence often seen in this process should not be sensationalised as being caused by 'evil spirits' or as proof that evil spirits exist, despite the religious views encouraging this point of view. In fact, it may be reasonable to say that Man would not have any concept of evil spirits without a history of religious prompting of this kind.

God – a balance of probabilities?

This was designed to support the particular religion's own agendas and also provided a convenient answer for the priesthood when confronted, for example, with those afflicted with mental illnesses – 'they were possessed of an evil spirit'.

Keep in mind that those in the priesthood were just as superstitious as their followers and when they had to find suitable explanations for inexplicable happenings, often had to fall back on the concept of evil spirits as the answer. It got them off the hook and sufficiently frightened their followers so that no further answers were required.

Uncontrolled energy activity, certainly, and there's the danger, but not an evil energy activity. These concepts are now so ingrained in Man's imagination that it will probably take some generations to remove them – if at all. This is not to say that these odd physical effects don't happen, just that the cause is wrongly identified.

Robert Rowe

CHAPTER SEVEN

Ethical Considerations

Having considered the spiritual factors applicable to living on Earth, we should now look at other factors that also affect our lives and may need redefining and/or comment, such as the 'why me?' cry.

Among other matters, this chapter discusses the effects of how and where we live, and suggests that we are all at risk to some degree as our lives are governed by choice and chance factors.

Right and Wrong

These terms are only of local importance relative to existing moral and civil law, both of which are variable and evolving and apply to life and living conditions of each individual at a particular time and in that particular society. This appears to be confirmed by looking at the variations that currently exist, nation to nation, and the variations that have occurred in recorded history.

It is not the intention to just dismiss these as of little value but simply to point out that they are variable facts of living that will affect us according to where we live at any particular time. Each of us deals with these according to our abilities as a part of our normal living functions.

Choice and Chance

The subject of Choice is self-explanatory and requires little further comment except to point out that the exercise of personal choice always has consequences which are largely predictable. Chance, on the other hand, whilst similar, can introduce subtle added variations that aren't always predictable. It is a part of reality and as errors in interpretation of specific experience are a normal part of being human, so interpretive variations, person to person, are also normal and to be expected.

For convenience, these points are considered here under two headings: a) environmental, that is, factors caused by how and where we live and the damage this causes, and b) personal factors caused by our individual make-up.

It will be seen that all of us are at some considerable risk brought about by the effects of these two factors and great care should be taken in making the choices that we do.

a) Environmental Aspects

Our lives are continually involved with making *choices* on where and how we will live and the conditions under which we live and, therefore, *we* create the types of *chances* that will affect our lives. Speaking both in a metaphorical sense as well as in a real sense, nearly all of us can choose whether, where, and when we are going to cross busy, or not so busy, highways of life.

God – a balance of probabilities?

If our *choice* causes us to cross more busy highways than is prudent, then the *chances* that an accident will occur are increased considerably. Again, if we choose to cross at more or less dangerous points, then so the chances of problems occurring will vary accordingly, and if we cross those highways at peak hour traffic, then the probability of an accident must be further increased. Similarly, the odds are varied enormously according to our individual ability to dodge traffic and this, of course, varies with age and health. That's a lot of *choices* and *chances*.

So, all of us are making decisions throughout our lives which, like crossing highways, can affect our wellbeing and it is not surprising if on occasion, when these decisions aren't as judicious as we would have liked, we have to suffer the results. Usually, these are of a minor nature and are part of our normal living experiences.

But some persons are better equipped, mentally and/or physically, to avoid the results of life's 'highway crossing' than others, and as this varies throughout their lifetimes, so accidents may or may not occur at particular times; it is a matter of individual *choice* in highway selection and *chance*, as to the type of incident and whether and when this is likely to occur.

It is important to note that each person can alter his chances of survival either way, by recognising his changed needs and abilities (age/health?) and altering his choices. For example, moving away from the highway, or the potentially hazardous decision, to a more suitable situation will automatically alter his survival chances, hopefully to his benefit. If he chooses not to do so, or makes a foolish choice, then it is unrealistic to seek to blame others for any misfortune that might occur.

b) Personal

When you think about it, all life is full of many sorts of uncertainties that breed real or imagined fears, which Man continually strives to overcome. In addition, all of us carry imperfections which, by and large, are not important, or which can be offset by various aids. For example, our eyes and ears don't work as well throughout our lifetime and we aid these by wearing glasses or hearing aids.

However, there are hidden imperfections that may cause organ failures under some circumstances that will vary according to the individual's general health and lifestyle, so that ulcers, heart failure or similar may occur suddenly and at random, or progressively, as wear and tear takes its toll. Again, *choice* and *chance* at work.

Where an individual has an accident causing an injury, or inherits a tendency to contract a particular type of health problem, then, at some particular time, this weakness may cause a breakdown of some sort to occur, without the individual contributing to its onset at all. It's simply a part of that person's make-up and unless some prior warning or information is available, completely unavoidable and only due to *chance* circumstances.

Think of the complex automatic chemical functions which our bodies carry out in food processing, the total length of veins (there are over 100,000 km of veins in the average adult body carrying blood around our bodies at varying pressures), and also the continual repair and replacement program in which our bodies are constantly engaged.

Think, also, of how our mental processes have to rely on all of these activities functioning correctly at all times, in order for us to live in an organised way. Any small weakness or error in these activities can be serious and who can say that a breakdown is not likely to occur at any time because of some inherent fault as yet unknown or unrecognised.

Finally, consider the effect of both environmental and personal circumstances working for or against us at any particular time and it will be seen that we all are, or can be, at considerable risk on a minute by minute basis, depending on how the *choice/chance combination* of all these circumstances works out.

All of us are aware of people who have devoted their lives to helping others, often at great personal risk, and who have died prematurely, and also of others who have caused great suffering to their fellow man and could be said to have lived too long. This is no-one's fault but simply the way in which the combination of that person's *choice and chance* circumstances have worked out under their living conditions – that is, the cumulative choice and chance circumstances where that person lived at that time.

The choice and chance points, perhaps, could be illustrated by using the German dictator, Hitler, as our example, when considering the events leading to the 1939–45 Second World War. Let's not think about the choice and chance situations which led to the first Great War, but just think about all of the choice and chance combinations which came about as a result of decisions following the first Great War (1914 to 1918).

A simplification is that the first Great War ended in the defeat of Germany in 1918, causing quite unrealistic burdens to be placed on that country, leading to a demoralised society and a delayed recovery for many years. This sowed the seeds for the rise of Hitler and the Nazi Party and causing Germany's eventual revival as an industrial nation based largely on military production. A different or a more enlightened choice of options after the Great War might well have avoided the Second World War of 1939–45.

We should accept that the conditions of choice and chance are the circumstances under which all species on Earth have evolved since creation – nothing is basically altered, we still carry out much the same basic functions required to live on Earth, although the cause of stresses may have altered. We are responsible for our own actions according to our choice/chance selections of activities.

Why Me?

Perhaps, at this point the 'why me?' question should be looked at. Many people are distressed because they were unharmed during some catastrophe, such as an earthquake or similar upheaval, or because of a war of some sort occurring, when others around them were killed or injured. The question asked is 'why me?' – 'why should I be spared when others have suffered?' or alternatively, 'what have I done to deserve this sort of terrible treatment?'

These questions are really examples of the individual trying to find explanations for the outcome of circumstances *over which he has no control* by blaming others, or by needlessly accepting fault or blame themselves. It is a confused emotional response to a problem which, on most occasions, is unanswerable. The question doesn't apply to the problem and could just as easily be 'why anyone?'

It's just the result of *chance circumstances* which caused us to be born with a particular set of inherited genes and/or being at a particular place at a particular time, and the 'why me?' cry, is really a cry for understanding and support in a time of great stress and confusion, resulting from a deep personal and emotional loss. It requires care and understanding of each other.

Environmental Care

It naturally follows from all of this that if, as suggested, there is only one 'living energy' common to all living things on Earth, then in addition to caring for his own life form, Man, as the dominant life force sharing this energy, has the onus, or responsibility, of caring for all other life forms on the Earth to provide for future generations.

It should be kept in mind that left undisturbed, these interacting balances tend to form a self- sustaining system and as such have the ability to accept vast changes of conditions over a period of time. But where conditions are changed too quickly, then some life forms may disappear and Man, as the main initiator of these types of changes, has the responsibility to ensure that in his efforts to survive, he doesn't inadvertently cause irreparable damage to the system overall.

Keep in mind, too, that our universe is a work in progress – that is, we are all a part of this developmental process that will continue for an indeterminate period of time.

A world set up so that human beings could emerge is known as an Anthropic Universe and as so many of the physical aspects of our solar system seem to be finetuned for this purpose, it is reasonable to suggest that the evolvement of the human race was probably inevitable. This is given particular emphasis by the 'Gaia' proposition.

Gaia – James Lovelock

The concept of Gaia was conceived by James Lovelock, a medical scientist charged with investigating problems involved in the search for life on Mars for NASA, and as a part of this investigation, had to think about life itself – what it is and what distinguishes it from nonlife.

He was aware that the Earth is continually engaged in repairing its inherent ecological systems and was struck by the similarity of these processes to those of living entities on Earth which constantly carry out similar tasks. Lovelock has called the totality of the living Earth, Gaia, the Greek name for Mother Earth.

In considering these matters:

He realised that Mars and Venus have atmospheres composed almost totally of carbon dioxide, with no free oxygen. In contrast, Earth's atmosphere has small amounts of carbon dioxide and is about 20% oxygen. Although oxygen is a highly reactive element and tends to be removed from the atmosphere by various organisms, including Mankind, plants continually release more oxygen to compensate for this loss.

Now, what is remarkable is that the level of oxygen has remained relatively constant over a long period of time despite the world's increase in human and animal population. For example, a small oxygen increase to perhaps 25% or 30% could cause the atmosphere to burst into flames, while a decrease to 10% would probably be lethal to most life forms.

Something has kept the amount of oxygen at just the right concentration for millions of years thus enabling the development of Mankind.

Further, Lovelock reasoned that the oceans became salty by the leaching of minute quantities of salt from rock and soil into rivers and streams that flow to the sea. Why, then, haven't the oceans become saltier and saltier? Similarly, why haven't rising levels of carbon dioxide increased the temperature on Earth? (Evidence of such an increase is now becoming obvious.)

On Venus, the carbon dioxide rich atmosphere has turned the planet into an oven. By contrast, the thin atmosphere of Mars, which is low in carbon dioxide, cannot retain heat, and so the planet is frigid.

Yet here on Earth the oceans haven't boiled away, even though the sun's intensity has increased by 25% since the sun was formed. Until recently, something has kept the temperature of Earth and the salt concentrations in the oceans relatively constant.

Lovelock's daring conclusion was that the total of all living things on Earth has somehow kept the concentration of carbon dioxide and oxygen, the amount of salt in the ocean and temperature constant. Not consciously or deliberately, but as a part of an automatic process, just as our bodies increase our heart rate when we exercise, or repair wounds when we are hurt.

But now technology has allowed us to generate massive quantities of greenhouse gasses far faster than Gaia's capacity to remove them and ecological changes are evident as a result. Eventually, compensatory changes may reduce carbon dioxide levels, but it should be kept in mind that, in the meantime, Gaia plays no favourites with which species will survive or disappear. It is the duty of Mankind to ensure that his greed for, and misuse of, the Earth's resources doesn't cause a catastrophic climate change. Given time, the Earth can probably recover, but this may be at the cost of the physical survival of Mankind.

CHAPTER EIGHT

Relationship with God

Now, having established our identity, our reason for being here and our relationship with others and with our world, the next point which has to be discussed is our relationship with God.

So, before proceeding with a relationship discussion, perhaps some comment should be offered on whether there is a God or not. This is something that each individual has to decide for himself, but it seems to me that if your Intelligent Self accepts that your Inner Self or the spiritual component of yourself exists, then it is also very reasonable to suggest that a spiritual world must exist as well. If this is so, then a belief that God exists is also reasonable.

It might be helpful to keep in mind that no matter how this subject is dressed up, God does not *'belong'* to any particular set of beliefs, or groups of people – Man simply hopes that by adopting specific religious beliefs he might be more acceptable to God, but, undoubtedly, this is a matter of opinion. Those coming from a religious background would probably say that God is everywhere, without really being able to define just what that means. Let me agree with this proposition that God is, indeed, everywhere, but in a spiritual sense.

There has been some suggestion from those who deny the existence of God, that life could be caused by some sort of spontaneous generation, but we then have to ask what originally caused this to happen and having sorted this out, to ask again what caused these particular factors to also come into being. Even a spontaneous generation requires something to have existed previously even if this only refers to a basic energy of some sort.

Perhaps the following comments might be helpful in thinking about these points. If most people are asked to describe God, they find it extremely difficult and usually fall back on the clichéd description advanced by various religious authorities. The fact that this description was invented by religious authorities, centuries ago, to provide a focal point for their religion and as an aid to the control of largely uneducated people, seems to have been overlooked.

It isn't possible to describe the indescribable in earthly terms, and apart from asserting that God must be a form of spiritual energy, it becomes a question without meaning – so how can an earthly relationship be formed with an indescribable spiritual energy force of which we can't begin to have any understanding? It's just not an acceptable concept.

Again, to those who feel that God would also be interested in our **physical** wellbeing, the question has to be asked why would this be so? As God has allowed Man to be knowledgeable enough to, by and large, control his physical world and his own physical wellbeing, why would God want to interfere? Within the limits of his knowledge, Man is in charge of his world and has to bear the consequences of his own actions.

God – a balance of probabilities?

Wouldn't it be more logical that God, as the supreme spiritual energy source, would have a greater interest in our spiritual wellbeing, rather than our temporary physical wellbeing?

Doesn't it also seem logical that if God decided to use disposable physical bodies as temporary hosts for spiritual entities, these spiritual entities would be made indestructible. That is, that they couldn't be harmed, regardless of what happened to the physical body.

Later in this discussion, it is proposed to more fully discuss the scientific view that all matter at its basic atomic level is energy and that this is a valid way of describing the Earth and all it contains, including all living species.

It is suggested here that this also includes spiritual energy and as all energy comes from the one source, in my view from God, this simply agrees with the proposition that God is everywhere in an energy sense and that a supreme Spirit or God must exist to have set it all in motion. A denial of the existence of God, then, seems to me to also suggest a denial of the existence of intelligent life and everything else – that is, that nothing really exists. But even a mirage is a form of energy that has to exist somewhere for it to be in existence. The proposition that energy exists automatically requires that a source for that energy must also exist.

However, there is one overriding aspect that has to be considered separately, because of its special innate quality. As a part of his spiritual heritage, Mankind has been imbued with an emotion that is an inbuilt deep feeling of concern for the welfare of others, to the point where, on special occasions, he will sacrifice his life to help them. I think this is the result of the influence of Mankind's Inner Self in a time of great need, that is acted upon usually to counteract a very real physical danger of some sort to others, perhaps caused by Man's own avarice, greed or hatred.

Our problems on Earth are of our own making, or are part of the evolution of the environment in which we live. We should, therefore, concentrate our efforts on the best way in which we can overcome these problems, rather than seeking to blame others, or looking to God for divine intervention.

We experience very few problems which do not fit into these categories, and this is borne out to a large degree by the number of innocent people who are killed, maimed, or starve through no fault of their own, when suitable prior action by themselves, or others, would have eased the problems involved.

Think of the Holocaust in Europe, the continuing problems in the Middle East, and the mass killings in Africa, S.E. Asia and South America. To blame God for a lack of action to correct the problems Man has caused in these areas is quite futile and unrealistic.

It is simply a matter of Man's willingness to help. That is to say, Man is in charge of his own morals, or way of thinking, and it is his choice whether he will or won't help his fellow man. The degree to which this occurs is a measure of the correctness of our approach to life's problems, and of how far we have to go to achieve a more ideal world. Under these circumstances it is quite unrealistic to try to relate our local problems and shortcomings back to being 'part of God's plan'. This point of view is an attempt to avoid responsibility for Man's local action or lack of action.

However, it should not be assumed that the lack of response to a plea for the easing or curing of suffering should be regarded as proof that there is no God. It seems more likely that God is not reachable in the way that has been supposed and encouraged over the centuries. I suggest that the basic flaws in most religious thinking are:
1) their insistence that a *personal relationship with God* (as prescribed by their religious tenets) can exist, and
2) their use of wrong interpretations of chance circumstances as proof of their claim.

Think about this a bit more. What type of relationship could we hope to have with an all- knowing, all-powerful Being, who would know our thoughts before we formed them? Would the expression of thoughts be necessary? Why would God bother? Mankind is in charge of his own destiny – the futility of the idea seems obvious.

Now, it is very understandable that the concept of an indirect relationship with God may be difficult to accept and would probably be rejected, because for centuries religions have perpetuated and used their emotional and personal Man/God relationship concept as an integral part of their hierarchical and belief statements. You may agree that this is, mainly, an effort to ensure the continuing future of these organisations by promoting this as a comforting element that their followers can also share.

But doesn't the concept of a *personal relationship with your own spiritual Inner Self* with its inbuilt indirect relationship with God seem to make more sense? Keep in mind that the individual has to also participate in this process – that is to acknowledge the Inner Self's existence – for the relationship to be successful. Doesn't it seem logical that each individual's spirit is in a better position, having access to that person's Intellect and being aware of any special needs, to cater for whatever that individual's needs are likely to be at any time?

Wouldn't this be more consistent with what we see happening in the world today, and provide a better explanation of why relief for Mankind's problems has always seemed to be haphazard and subject to variation through the centuries? It's no wonder that relief has been unpredictable – it has always depended on human relationships which, at best, were subject to variation and instability from time to time.

For example, can you offer details of any recent happening in the world which can be attributed, *without question*, to the direct intervention of God? No, not the sort of thing where somebody claims to have been instructed, or told, by God to do something, or to follow a particular path. This could just as easily be a choice based on a deep rooted opinion, or feeling, which surfaced at that particular time and which, nevertheless, turned out to be most beneficial (or otherwise!).

Of course, it is possible, as we have already discussed, that somebody's Inner Self may have influenced such a decision, but the point is that no-one else can confirm this independently. Similarly, we are not speaking of earthquakes and other natural disasters – these are a part of the physical world in which we live and statistics can be provided to both prove and disprove anything you like. We are talking about a public 'parting of the waters of the Red Sea' stuff, or even a not so grand undertaking, which is undeniably the hand of God in action.

There have been plenty of human catastrophes, opportunities if you like, happening in recent years – the Holocaust to name an obvious one – which would have warranted such a direct intervention.

Isn't this lack of activity then consistent with the point of view that God has little or no interest in the **physical** welfare of the human race? I suggest that it is reasonable to put forward the view that God sorted out the laws of physics and conditions needed for the Universe to develop, and then left it for its occupants to take advantage of, or not. As far as we can tell, God has taken no further part in its operation as it is complete of itself, and the physical progress of the inhabitants of each world will depend on their abilities to grow mentally, physically and spiritually.

But, hang about – what about all of the seemingly inexplicable happenings which occur from time to time – those interventions in the affairs of Man which are commonly said were God's will, or that God caused this or that to happen? Well, apart from natural causes, isn't there another option?

Isn't it possible that this is an example of the choice and chance factors discussed earlier? Isn't it also reasonable to assume that the combined spiritual efforts of those involved with the particular happening may have something to do with it? A combination of all sorts of influences? Perhaps on this occasion contact with the 'collective unconscious', referred to earlier, pointed the way to or provided the answer?

You will note that I have used the word 'assume' and this is all that we can do. In the absence of the availability of facts, we can only seek a reasonable answer to a question , which can't be answered conclusively. But, we shouldn't avoid accepting a reasonably based answer - that is ' a balance of probabilities' approach - simply because it upsets previously held beliefs.

It is a part of the chain of knowledge yet to be ascertained, but the important aspect is that if it is more reasonable than any other improbable hypothesis offered to date, why should we ignore the possibilities it raises? Why should we be expected to continue to accept any notions that have had centuries to be proven, but are still highly unreliable?

Yes, I know it's probably more acceptable and comfortable to fit in with most religious views and claim that this or that was a result of divine intervention, but think about it a bit more – isn't there another reason closer to home? Given that God also supervises the Universe and must be fairly busy, isn't it more likely that any, if you like, supernatural or other than natural happenings are the result of coincidence or local on-the-spot, combined spiritual efforts?

Isn't it reasonable to say that those who are striving to achieve a particular outcome will be spiritually hoping, praying or meditating – that is contacting God indirectly via their own Inner Selves/Souls – for this outcome to occur, and that on this occasion, the combined efforts caused it to happen? The 'collective unconscious' in action.

Doesn't this explain the apparent haphazard nature of these types of happenings? Sometimes our efforts aren't as correct as we would have liked, and we have to suffer the results.

Usually, these are of a minor nature and are part of our normal living experiences.

Need for Religion

When you think about this a little, you will have to agree that a religion really is a belief system that is imposed on us by others, *after we are born*. We are already equipped with an Inner Self (Soul) at that time, so a religious belief as such, has no bearing on its existence, or otherwise. Your Inner Self is a part of your natural inheritance as a human being whether you acknowledge it or not.

It may seem that the subject of Man's relationship to God is so mysterious and basic, that only those versed in certain ways of thinking are able to offer the 'correct path'. But the record of past achievements by those supposedly well versed in their religious views is not very encouraging and suggests that a different approach might be worth considering.

What Is a Religion?

I suppose a good place to start, then, would be to try to define what we are talking about when we refer to a 'religion', and a reasonable definition might be to say that it is an organised program of beliefs, rites and ceremonies that, it is hoped, will lead to a closeness with that religion's view of God. However, it is also reasonable to say that these same rites and ceremonies were also ritual devices used for the subjugation of the individual to the prevailing view of the religious authorities then in power.

In the beginning, these statements and rites were propounded by an individual as having been handed down authoritatively from 'above' or from 'within', and it is indisputable that these statements and rites are his interpretation of what the correct approach to God should be. Now, this is fine and there can be no argument about this, it was that individual's view of the correct procedure to be adopted and it may well have been for him at that time.

But, taking this further, the fact that it had been adopted by a group of like minded people, translated into a number of different languages, and reinterpreted and amended by various scholars over the centuries, allows room for many errors and, in any case, doesn't alter the fact that it was originally just one person's opinion.

It just isn't possible to establish beyond reasonable doubt that religions are anything but a matter of opinion established by those interested in the continuance of a specific regime of practices. It is understood this viewpoint requires the discarding of centuries of teaching, and it may be almost impossible to immediately switch to the adoption of a quite different and, perhaps for some, radical way of thinking for themselves. But, it is probably beneficial for everyone, at an appropriate stage in their lives, to stand back and examine their religious beliefs in the same way that other aspects of living are tested. If they are found wanting, then it is up to the individual to try to establish facts, based on today's circumstances, and live their lives accordingly.

God – a balance of probabilities?

Of course, as has been said earlier, due acknowledgment must be made of the beneficial aspects which have helped to establish the basis of our society today, so that we don't lose sight of these benefits. But it seems unreasonable to continue to accept stories of events which may have happened many centuries ago and have been reported and translated a number of times since (maybe distorted) and which bear little relationship to today's facts, as a basis for today's living.

Religions, which mystify and confuse their adherents to support the need for their advices and pronouncements, have really removed the basis for their own existence. After all, we are discussing the progress and development of the most important part of our lives, the Inner Self, on its way through life here and now and on to whatever may lie beyond, and it must be indisputable that we should use the best possible basis we can find on which to chart our course.

If we now look at this seriously, there is, of course, a great mystery about God and the human spirit that with our present knowledge is beyond our understanding. But, as has been pointed out earlier, there is no mystery about how to contact the human spirit and God, and no need for any great ceremony to be observed, apart from those that you decide are necessary for yourself.

An example of this could be to take the instance of someone living far away from civilization, without formal religious beliefs. Is his sincere invocation to God any less acceptable because he doesn't have the benefit of a ritual or indulge in some particular ceremony? Surely not. Isn't it more important that the correct attitude of mind is observed at that time? Isn't this also the basis of any hoped for contact with God? Your success or otherwise will be the measure of whether you need to alter your approach or not. This will probably include a form of meditation – or inward dialogue – which could be said to be a form of prayer, as this is the basis of contact with your spiritual or Inner Self.

If the truth was really known, it is quite probable that we are all in touch with our Inner Selves more often than we realise. Every time we make a serious decision involving our basic wellbeing or the wellbeing of others, or a decision involving morals, seems to be an opportunity for an internal dialogue. This can happen unconsciously or consciously, but is more effective if it is a conscious act, as determined by the individual.

It can be said that when you contact your Inner Self you are, in effect, opening the door to the possibility of indirect contact with God, and this can be done simply and at a time and place that you find is most suitable or necessary. It's your choice – no-one can force you to do this – it has to be born of the individual's inner needs and whether he will allow these to surface or not.

Proof of the effectiveness or otherwise of this contact will be shown by changes in the individual's behaviour. That is, you can't make a continuing meaningful contact with your Inner Self without some changes to your own physical and mental outlook occurring. As you are not following any complex rules laid down by others, you don't need any 'professionals' to oversee that you are carrying these out correctly. You will know yourself of any deficiencies.

Finally, any real or imagined sins are wrongs carried out by the physical Self in a physical world against (usually) another physical person, and as the physical body will eventually die, it is important that these wrongs are sorted out and corrected before this happens. The correction of earthly wrongs is essentially an earthly function not a spiritual function, but may, however, be suggested by spiritual interaction.

But, the concept of God taking vengeance against an obviously lesser being at the end of his physical life is, in my view, offensive, as it suggests that God would be petty enough to behave in this way.

Keep in mind that, as your spirit is already of God and indestructible, you can't be lost and don't need to be saved. It should be noted that this doesn't preclude the possibility of the need for the correction of wayward beliefs after death and when in the spiritual realm. Keep in mind, too, that the absence of a religious belief need not, and does not, lessen Man's spirituality in any way, as this is an inherent part of his birthright.

It has been shown that religions are man-made and are based on opinions which, at best, are likely to be influenced by the mythology of the times. So in summary, then, religions are only as important as YOU wish to make them or as YOU are prepared to allow others to impose on you. Remember, religious texts and writings were written many years after events took place for largely uneducated people and cannot be taken as a literal history of those events.

To be expected to accept these now is not good enough for today's world. It really gets back to your view of God and what you think is required. Given the discussion here, and using a balance of probabilities approach, which religions do you feel are the right ones to follow and what do you think God thinks of all these competing variations?

Selective Spiritualism

There are many practitioners who have investigated specialised aspects of spiritual energy and these may be of interest, but keep in mind that these pathways might display a lack of stability unless guided by an experienced person. It might be considered that, rather than following a biased side issue that seems attractive for the moment, a general, more balanced spiritual approach to God, as the provider of all spiritual energy, might be preferable. However, this is for the individual to decide.

An Overall View

My view of God is supported by history, and is that of a supreme spiritual Being, who having set in process the creation of the universe and all that it holds and having given Mankind the wit and intelligence to survive and develop on his world, has then stood aside. If Mankind despoils his world so that it becomes uninhabitable, then Man will have also destroyed himself physically, in my view, proving his unworthiness for the task.

Spiritually, Man is made in God's image – that is, he is primarily a spiritual being, appearing as a physical being in order to live on an apparent physical Earth. At death he passes back into his spiritual state for whatever lies ahead.

God – a balance of probabilities?

Look, it's your choice, you are responsible for your relationship with God – no-one else can be involved at this level, so isn't a simple and sincere, direct relationship with God's local agent– your Inner Self (Soul) – more realistic?

Keep in mind, this doesn't preclude a group approach, if you so wish, with like-minded people, but the above proposition doesn't alter – you are responsible for your own actions and are independent of uncertain propositions from ages past that have little relevance today.

However, if existing religious thinking is acceptable or preferable, then there is little more to be said – but you will keep thinking about it, won't you? It gets back to the standard of proof that the individual requires for a belief system on which to shape his life.

Up until now, Mankind has been required to have faith in a belief system that is based on the interpretation of ancient writings. These writings, centuries old, have led to a multiplicity of confusing and competing religions and practices on which to establish a belief in the existence of God.

But, there is now an alternative choice to be examined and perhaps accepted. This is today's theoretical but accepted concept of the one universal energy that pervades the universe, that, it is suggested, can also allow for spiritual energy and a belief in the existence of God. It's your choice.

Robert Rowe

PART FOUR

Reconciliation between Science and Philosophy

Is Science the mathematics of Philosophy? Are Science and Philosophy the two ends of the same stick? A reconciliation between these opposite ends is proposed and imagination (or reality?) is unleashed.

Robert Rowe

CHAPTER NINE

At its most basic level, the study of Science is the study of energy and all that it entails, and as our Life Force is a form of energy that is described by Philosophy, then Science and Philosophy are closely related and a new overall discipline, PhiloScience, may be justified.

Quantum Theory

According to Quantum Physics, Matter doesn't exist. Historically, Physicists thought that matter consisted of compounds of various elements which in turn are made up of various atoms consisting of energy. From this, Matter is really a form of energy and as mental processing is also a form of energy then it is reasonable that these two energy forms can be interactive

The proposition is put forward that as the universe is composed of energy, Man is, in fact, an energy being, who appears as a physical being for the purpose of living on an apparent physical Earth and reverts back to a spiritual energy being at death.

In effect, Energy Man = Physical Man at birth = Energy Man at death. Energy is conserved – nothing is destroyed, only changed. It may well be that the death of an individual in one part of the universe allows the birth of another individual in another part of the universe.

This chapter discusses how Man processes his existence mentally and points out that, of all concepts of the past, present and future, only the 'present' is 'real' in the temporary physical sense. In a fraction of a second the continuing present becomes the continuing past. So, as reality is constantly changing with the passing of time, a continuing re-evaluation of the present reality is required to assess present dangers and/or difficulties to be overcome. This is our normal practice of living in 'today's' world.

Scientific Compatibility

This section follows on from earlier suggestions that Man can be viewed as a spiritual energy entity and offers some comments in support of the idea of the probable close compatibility of Science and Philosophy.

Proving conclusively that Philosophy and Science are each a part of a larger body of knowledge (PhiloScience?) is beyond the scope of this work, but if the range of probabilities of each discipline is extended toward the other, then perhaps a more universally complete language, and an added understanding of our world and its place in the universe, will result.

It is also appropriate to remember that in earlier days, most of those who investigated scientific matters were, in fact, religiously inspired philosophers, so that Religion and Science do have a co-operative past and the suggested name of PhiloScience is not far from the mark. Consider the following.

Science has informed us that all matter is made up of atoms that, at basic levels, consist of electrical charges (electrons etc.) and space in various combinations, so all materials common to our world – air, rocks, wood, metals, gases, liquids, minerals and salts etc. – can be shown to be various combinations of atoms (energy) that exist to create those particular materials. Now, as we are made up of these same types of atoms, this generalisation also applies to us.

As has been indicated earlier, a general assessment of the body is that it contains about 70% water, 18% bone, 10% fat/tissue etc. with the remaining 2% consisting mainly of a mixture of minerals, metals, salts of various types and so on. All of these can be listed in terms of their atomic content. For an obvious example, water consists of H_2O – that is, 2 atoms of Hydrogen and 1 atom of oxygen – so that the body's content of water, bone (calcium) and fat (oils), minerals, metals and salts can similarly be described in terms of individual atomic energy content. We are energy beings.

Nanotechnology

In more recent days, research has led to the establishment of Nanotechnology – broadly, the study of how matter can be controlled at an atomic level – which raises the possibility of telepathy and even teleportation – the movement and creation of objects by non-physical means. While the creation of matter from the assembly of specific atoms for inert materials can now be carried out experimentally, there is little doubt in my mind, that this will eventually lead to the renewal of body parts and, additionally, will probably lead to a better control of disease.

However, it should be kept in mind that the very essence of being human is in the Inner Self and Life Force that powers it. Both of these are non-physical energy processes that need different, though related, approaches.

Energy

Now, let's be clear about what we are trying to do. We are endeavouring to show that the scientific and spiritual views of energy are in many ways similar and complementary, and it could reasonably be suggested that, with a little push, the discussion is about the one and same overall subject, but from differing points of view.

The following summary will be helpful.

1. Man's physical characteristics can be reduced to cellular structure and viewed in terms of their atomic **energy** content.

2. Man's very existence depends on sensory **energy** signals – sight, sound, touch, smell, taste – provided to his Intellect for identification and **energy** memory storage.

3. Man's very existence also depends on his use of intellectual **energy** to process this information – to think about and separately, as appropriate, to generate **energy** to enable physical action.

4. That Man exists at all as a living entity is proof of the existence of a 'Life Force' that is a form of **energy**.

God – a balance of probabilities?

It is suggested here that consciousness/Intellect is an undoubted part of the Life Force, and it is also suggested that it has access to a spiritual **energy** entity, an Inner Self, as discussed in Chapter 6.

You may say that this latter is unproven and a matter of opinion and you are correct, but only because another individual's personal standard of proof, for matters of this kind, is usually unacceptable as a universal proof. Science has yet to devise a universally acceptable **spiritual energy** measuring device, but even if this component is ignored, based on the fact of being alive, Physical Man = Energy Man.

With the above in mind, any discussion about the basic nature of matter has to accept that there is a borderline over which the discussion about physical characteristics becomes a discussion about energy. The two aspects are differing views about the same entity.

There is nothing odd or new about this – it has always been so, but perhaps it hasn't been pointed out before in this context. Of course, both views are correct, it depends on how you look at the subject – if broad physical needs are involved then it's pointless discussing atomic structure, but if basic energy values are to be discussed then our special electron microscope is required to view ourselves at this level.

In other words, we are both physical and energy beings at the same time, depending on how we are viewed. It is probably worthwhile at this point, to emphasise that the suggested 'energy' view is not a denial of our physical existence, but is really the start of an acknowledgement that a view of ourselves other than a physical view is also a valid way of self-observance.

If taking other than a physical view of ourselves seems a bit odd, it might be of interest to consider that we already do this, selectively, for inert substances as a part of our normal living experience. For example, water, a staple part of our existence, can be viewed in four different ways depending on circumstances – as water which we view as fluid and temperate, ice which we view as hard and cold, steam which is warm and nebulous, and finally as energy, H_2O. All of these views are regarded as quite normal depending on prevailing conditions and requiring the addition or depletion of energy.

My point here is that the conscious viewing of ourselves in energy terms can be seen to be in line with normal living conditions if we accept that without a Life Force we also would be the inanimate objects consisting of water, calcium, fats, metals, salts, etc. of which the Earth is made.

A further confirmation that we are energy beings is provided by the fact that when energy in the form of focused magnetic beams is applied to parts of the brain, a temporary disruption can be caused to the body's physical functions. This is the result of an interaction between the neuromagnetic fields inherent in the minute electrical currents (energy) generated by the brain and the focused magnetic beam. A further example is the speeding up of healing of a wound by magnetic therapy – this is an interaction between an applied magnetic field and the inherent neuromagnetic field at a basic cellular atomic level.

God – a balance of probabilities?

As with emerging therapies, varying results are achieved depending on the approach being taken by the participants and this is discussed very fully by Charles Polk and Elliot Postow in their revision of the effects of magnetic fields in the *Handbook of Biological Effects of Electromagnetic Fields*.

The efficacy of this treatment is not a part of this discussion, but simply confirms that as the body is composed of elements (atoms, protons, electrons etc.) that provide the neuromagnetic fields (energy), and can be affected by other magnetic fields, it is very reasonable to say that Physical Man can quite correctly be described as an energy being.

Both views – Energy Man and Physical Man – are correct, but of these two views the energy view is the critical and ultimate form of existence because all physical forms depend on the mix of energy at the atomic level for their form and characteristics. This energy 'mix' is a man, this mix is a bird, this is an animal, this a tree, a rock, minerals, metal, liquid, a gas and so on.

To provide a degree of validation for this point of view, science advises us that the basic unit of matter or energy is known as a quanta. This is much smaller than the smallest atom and at this level Quantum Theory states that under the right conditions, matter and energy can become interchangeable.

You will recall the earlier comment about Einstein's Theory of Relativity, which confirms that, basically, mass can be equated to a quantity of energy under certain conditions. So it is very reasonable to also say that 'Physical Man' can, under the right circumstances, be seen to be 'Energy Man'. Certainly, Man appears as a physical being but might not this be for the sole purpose of existing on an apparent physical world? A sort of grand illusion?

You may be aware of the passage in the Bible which refers to the wise man, that is, a man with special knowledge and understanding who, in referring to the competition in our minds between the search for physical or spiritual possessions, says 'vanity, vanity – all is vanity', or a matter of opinion. Isn't this another way of saying that ultimately, 'all physical possessions are as nothing or of little value' – that is, that ultimately they are illusory?

Could this be a hidden confirmation that the physical aspects of our existence and of the Earth are not as they seem and are an illusory concept? Let those with eyes see, those with ears hear, and those with understanding, understand.

Perhaps we are programmed at conception into considering ourselves as physical beings when, in fact, this may not be so and we need reprogramming, for example when we die, to achieve our true form as a spiritual energy entity.

It may be that our form has to appear as a physical being to fulfil our life purposes on a physical Earth and to protect us from our true spiritual reality, until we can show that we are sufficiently enlightened mentally by our earthly apprenticeship, to accept our true condition.

Keeping in mind that Science agrees that under some circumstances, matter and energy are interchangeable, then physical reality is subjective and not necessarily the only 'real' view. This then helps to explain why the concepts of the Present, Past and Future are really forms of multiple parallel existences, taking no physical space at all except for those in current physical occupation. Of course, this couldn't be our true reality ... or could it?

Remember the UK Astronomer Royal, Sir Martin Rees, and his comments about multiple universes? He thinks it's **necessary in order to make sense of our apparent** physical condition. They have no relevance otherwise. If this scenario is given some thought it will be seen that a non-physical form would allow enough space on Earth to be a possibility for all time.

If you feel that this can't be taken seriously, simply because you can see and feel that we are physical beings living in a physical world, then you may like to consider the way that the effects of hypnosis, for example, can change our perceptions of reality, as discussed in previous paragraphs.

To recap, you would appear as a one-armed person to a hypnotised mind – the hypnotised person will be adamant that this is so, despite the fact that both your arms are clearly visible to others. He could, in fact, be induced to not be able to see a particular individual or object at all, and is a prime example of how easy it is to alter the way the mind interprets reality.

We've suggested that hypnosis is just a way of fooling our minds into thinking in 'impossible' terms, thereby showing how fragile our grasp of reality really is, but what if it could be a way of triggering our minds into seeing reality as it really is – not a physical world at all but an energy world.

Perhaps you should give this aspect further thought, in particular when considering those who claim to be able to see visions or spiritual entities. Their vision may be temporarily enhanced.

It may well be that we are not yet advanced enough (or mentally strong enough) to be able to handle this emotionally. This energy view would still fit in with the scientific view that all matter consists of electrical charges and space – think about that a bit more – maybe the acts of physically seeing and feeling aren't the infallible guides we think they are.

As has been discussed, these experiences are our mental energy interpretations of what we think is happening, and the acceptance of this as an energy view only seems impossible because we are indoctrinated into not accepting any other concept than that of having a physical form!

But for the moment, let's get right away from that viewpoint and ask the question – is all of the above a kind of sleight-of-hand trickery, or does it have some other important value to us all? Because if the above is true, then it can almost be said that Science, in establishing the concepts of atomic energy and Quantum Theory, is also providing a kind of support for the concept of 'Energy Man' living on an 'energy planet'. Not proof, mark you, but support ...?

Certainly, if Science can say, with authority, that this is an impossibility, then we should re- examine other non-scientific evidence to ascertain whether we should change our views or not. But it should be kept in mind that it is a very complex subject and really requires more detailed discussion than can be provided here to make a definitive decision. This complexity is unavoidable and you are asked to persevere with this to see whether you feel that it makes a kind of sense to you.

We've established the probability that Physical Man is Energy Man, but there is yet another obvious aspect that has to be considered and brought to account – the possibility of the existence of 'spiritual energy'.

Spiritual Energy

Science can confirm that a person is alive by observance and measurement of his vital signs, and the fact that his vital signs can be measured is proof that his Life Force is in existence. But Science can't measure what that Life Force consists of except to postulate that it is probably a form of energy. The manifestation of spiritual energy is dependent on the acknowledgement of the person's intellect, that it exists as a part of his natural heritage to assist in his lifetime development, and without this association Mankind will probably degrade and eventually disappear.

Robert Rowe

CHAPTER TEN

We now come to the fourth part of our journey – taking a step into the unknown by further examining the proposition that Man already has the innate characteristics of a spiritual being. To do this, we need to examine those factors that are essential to Man's existence at a very basic level, keeping in mind that energy of one sort or another is involved as a basic building block for everything on Earth and, as far as we can tell, everything in the universe also. We also need to acknowledge that speculation has a part in our discussion.

Energy Processing

As an inhabitant of an energy based universe, it will be no surprise that chief among Man's abilities are those necessary to process energy in all its forms. All of our senses are set up to transmit energy signals to our Intellect for interpretation, and it is the Intellect that is telling us what it is experiencing in terms of sight, sound, touch, taste, smell and so on, based on its processing of these living energy impulses and its mental records.

These records are fairly static, but are usually updated automatically, without conscious effort, according to our education and the general view of the environment in which we live. We are, therefore, continually satisfying our need to be reassured of the normality of our situation, to enable us to live in a changing world, by constantly upgrading our internal mental records.

But it should be said at the outset that there are a number of theories on how the mind works and no complete agreement exists on which is correct. Probably a mix of them all, to some degree, and it should be clearly understood that any comment here is of a general nature and subject to expert correction. Any variations will not alter the main thrust of our discussion.

As a starting point, and as a couple of examples, it will be obvious that to see requires, first, that an object exists to be seen, and second, the act of seeing. To hear requires that there is something to be heard, and second, the act of hearing, and this duality applies to all of our sensing abilities.

In each case, these are two separate processes, but each is also a part of the other. So, for example, we generate the energy sensations involved in the acts of seeing and hearing within our eyes and ears, to be sent via the nervous system for identification by the Intellect. This also applies to the Intellect itself, because for the Intellect to think requires that there is an Intellect and something to think about or to evaluate in some way.

A good example of this is to consider the emotions – when we are angry or happy, we have to have something to be angry or happy about. That is, the feeling of anger or happiness and the observance of those emotions are both mental energy processes that are a part of our Intellect. We *are* that anger or happiness because we are generating those energy sensations within ourselves. We *decide* whether we are happy or sad or angry.

God – a balance of probabilities?

The thought itself is a registration of consciousness of some event that has happened or is about to happen, or of some idea that is forming, but it's the emotional value we *choose* to place on that thought that causes our emotional involvement with the happening or idea. The Intellect is *choosing* to experience and to identify its own feelings against a chosen scale, as an automatic process of mental energy that occurs, usually without conscious effort.

However, feelings are often clothed with what we perceive as reality, or whatever is acceptable as reality at the time, but ultimately, as our perception is deepened, the truth is uncovered, confirming our feelings, or not, as the case may be. This is a final stage in our thinking, leading to a conclusion of some sort prior to its mental storage, perhaps requiring physical energy to be activated.

The third process involved in this is the way that the Intellect carries out the work of knowing how to interpret the sensations being received from the eyes, ears and/or other sensory organs.

An interesting point of view has been expressed by many scientists, who have shown that, in their opinion, the Intellect interprets or translates everything it sees, hears, feels and senses in accordance with a type of calculus mathematical formula. That is, it adopts a formulaic way of processing the signals it receives from the senses.

Apparently, when looking at an object, the original images are not stored as 'pictures', but the Intellect filters or interprets these images by the use of these formulae as waveforms or digital calculations to be stored as a memory. These are then recombined, in accordance with these formulae, when we visualise or remember the object.

To try to test this theory, various patterns were, apparently, converted to simple energy waveforms based on calculus formulae and it was found that the visual cortex brain cells responded to these simple waveform patterns in the same way as when looking at the original patterns.

This strongly suggests that this was the process the Intellect used in interpreting the various signals it received (and remembered). It should be said again that this point of view was not accepted by all scientists, but there is little doubt that it explains many aspects of how the Intellect works.

When a particular object is to be remembered or recognised, the Intellect searches for a similar energy waveform or pattern in memory for comparison purposes, and then using the appropriate mathematical formula, generates the particular image relative to this object to appear in the mind's eye for recognition to take place. If there are differences, then a new energy waveform is generated to be stored in the memory as an additional or replacement image.

As an aside, the comparison of this natural process with that in use by computers, in the storage of information is quite remarkable.

So, all of this adds up to the fact that, at a very basic level, we are a very 'frequency energy waveform' or 'cycle of happenings' conscious race of beings and it is not too much to say that cyclical energy waveforms are a fundamental to our very existence.

Cyclical Energy

To clarify this terminology a little – everything on Earth is keyed into cyclical energy functioning and is influenced by cycles of happenings or events, or even vibrations if you prefer. Consider the following basics – the Earth cycles around the sun at a set rate giving us a complete cycle of hot and cold seasons each year. The Earth spins (cycles) on its axis once every 24 hours, giving us a cycle of light and darkness each day.

Because Man is born on Earth, it is reasonable that he would be affected by fundamental earthly rhythms and influences and as the Earth is part of the universe and subject to its laws, he is affected by these also. It may well be that as our mode of living moves away from following these natural laws, our ability to 'tune in' to spiritual sources of assistance is markedly reduced, to our detriment.

This is shown to some degree by the relief experienced by stressed individuals who achieve a measure of renewal, or are helped to refocus their lives again, by undergoing meditation or similar mental relaxation exercises at quiet locations or 'retreats', or at places of spiritual focus, such as temples, churches etc.

It will be seen, therefore, that the above scenario provides for a very wide range of individual spiritual and mental growths over varying time scales throughout Man's lifetime, and as a superficial look at our world seems to confirm that this is what occurs, a cyclical energy view of our world and all that it contains, including Mankind, is a reasonable viewpoint to have.

To take this further – our hearing and vision use cyclical energy waveforms to function. What we hear as sound are cyclical pressure variations in the atmosphere that are converted to energy waveforms – in space you would hear nothing. Our eyes react to certain other waveforms that we call light, provided by the sun – at night-time when our source of light has gone below the horizon we have difficulty in seeing. Our ears and eyes transmit these signals as electrical waveforms to the Intellect for recognition of what is being seen or heard.

The point of these comments is to clearly establish that our very existence depends on our mental ability to interpret our world in terms of its cycles of energy happenings. After all, you can prove to yourself that this basic premise is accurate by monitoring the use of your eyes, ears, and senses of smell and touch etc. Using sight as an obvious example, you will appreciate our dependence on the colours green and red as safety/danger signals.

A point that should now be mentioned is that any attempted explanation of Man's existence, quite correctly has to face up to all sorts of situations that test its validity, and these can't be ignored simply because they may seem extreme or fanciful. Please consider the following.

It has been suggested that our eyes and ears can only respond to about 50% of the energy waveforms available and if this seems an unlikely suggestion, then an obvious question would be to ask how many infrared or ultraviolet waveforms have you seen lately? Not many, I'm sure, as these types of waveforms are outside the range of our vision. And what about the hearing and vision of animals and birds? We know they can see/hear things that we can't, so another question arises as to whether other waveforms or entities exist, that we can't see or hear?

We accept as fact that it is quite normal for us to be surrounded by radio and TV energy waveforms, for example. We can't see or feel them, but because suitable receivers have been developed to enable us to 'see/hear' the results of their processing, we are happy to accept their invisibility. But what about the spiritual waveforms or images that people claim to have seen or heard? Does the fact that the ability to see/hear these effects is not universal mean that a spiritual world doesn't exist?

It may well be that spiritual energy in the form of reported visions – ghosts if you wish – that some people encounter on occasion are the result of that person's hearing or vision being temporarily extended to take in an extra energy dimension from the past or the future. This may also explain clairvoyance.

Reality

Reality is what the reality is at a particular instant in time for each individual, and if that coincides with others' views of reality, then a communal view of reality has been established in which all can participate and remember. But keep in mind that it is a coincidence of a number of individual arrangements of energy values/time. The instant you break away from a communal view, then the individual's view of reality takes precedence, and reality is what the reality is for that individual at that instant.

A discussion on reality has its problems and it might be helpful if our earlier comments, that physical items can also be interpreted as quantities of energy, are kept in mind. The body's senses interpret the original event as an electrical waveform and store it, as such, for later use. If we can recall it later, we can say it has been remembered.

So what is the difference between an item that was originally interpreted as a quantity of energy for memory storage and the remembered energy waveform? How do you know which is the original and which is the copy? – both the original vision and the remembered vision are electrical waveforms.

You may say that you handled something, so you know that it is real. Could I remind you that your sense of touch also provided electrical waveform signals to your Intellect to be combined with the visible image to identify it as a whole, and stored the signal as such in your memory.

The decision about reality is made when both images are considered as being identical with the recorded image.

They are both interpreted energy waveform signals. If those signals are recreated from your memory to your mind's eye such as when you remember it – that is, the same process but in reverse – then is the article also real again? Yes, it certainly seems so when it is a part of a dream sequence, but it's still only a mental picture – so was it ever real? How do you know? What's the ultimate test that confirms reality? Consider the following:

God – a balance of probabilities?

1. All human reactions – sensory feelings (touch, smell, sight, hearing), thinking, reasoning, memory and so on are based on electrical energy discharges via nerve cells to the brain for the Intellect to examine, identify, and selectively store as an energy quotient in the memory. But a hypnotised person – assuming he has seen and handled a brick previously – can also be induced to 'feel and see' a brick that isn't there in front of him.

Perhaps the following somewhat lighthearted approach might help to summarise the position.

Q. So, which is real? The perceived electrical energy (vision, sound, feeling, etc.) when you originally looked at the brick at that time, or the stored electrical energy representation (vision, sound, feeling etc.) in the memory? What's the difference that makes this decision? They are both a part of the brain's functions and are identical electrical energy waveforms.

2. As stated earlier, the human body consists of about 70% water (H_2O), 18% bone, 10% fat etc. and 2% minerals etc. All of these can be expressed in atomic terms or as bundles of energy.

Q. How do you know you are a physical being? Yes, I know, silly question – but stop and think about it – Einstein's Theory of Relativity ($E=MC^2$) suggests that under some circumstances it need not be so. Back to the question – which are you, a physical body or an energy being, and importantly – how do you know?

Now take this slowly – if it is acceptable that we might be energy beings, it's also possible that we are born indoctrinated into thinking of ourselves as physical beings in order to live on an apparent physical Earth when in reality we are energy beings. This also allows for spiritual energy beings to exist, if you wish to think in theological or philosophical terms.

It's all in the mind you know ... the illusion of physical existence starts at birth and ends at physical death but the energy content goes on to whatever lies ahead.

My view is that we are energy beings living on and in an energy world, as it provides an explanation for all facets that we encounter during our living cycle, including a belief in God and an afterlife, if this is our opinion, and provides a rational meeting point for both Science and Philosophy.

So, the questions are, 'Are you there?' and 'How do you know?' and whether you are game enough to stand aside from convention to answer them with confidence and see yourself differently. Of course, these are of an academic nature and can be ignored as not of importance to our everyday living, if you wish, but, nevertheless, are there for the individual's decision.

Concepts of Present, Past and Future

The ability to experience or to be aware of concepts of the present, the past and the future is a vital part of the confirmation of our existence as physical beings. These concepts are terms we use every day to describe our experiences, and we place great reliance on our memories to keep them in some sort of relative order, so that we are able to make sense of our existence over time.

But it can be shown that only the present is really relevant in the sense that our physical senses are sending energy signals to our Intellect telling us that the present is here, right at this instant and needs to be dealt with. However, we need our memories and imagination to provide background energy 'pictures' in a certain way, in order to make sense of our expectations of our daily living.

It is reasonable, then, to emphasise that everything we do from the instant of birth onwards is based on our ability to perceive our needs at that time, and to put into effect the concepts of choice and chance. Mental energy options are presented to us, from which we make choices that are influenced by our past experiences, present needs and future aspirations. The selected energy choice then encapsulates the chance factors that will apply to that particular selection.

This is a continuing process throughout our lives and is similar to the Buddhist teaching which refers to life unfolding as a continuing seamless process, or flow of events, whereby a selected energy future with its attendant factors is brought towards us to become the present experience, before retreating into the energy past. It is a never-ending process which is only interrupted by death – a final human physical closing down process which, in my opinion, then leads into a spiritual existence.

1. Present – The Only True Reality

Keep in mind that the elusive and constantly self-inventing present is the only true reality we are likely to experience as physical beings, and that this ever-present moment becomes the past even as it is being measured or experienced. Its importance, of course, lies in the fact that it is also the time when decisions affecting our choice of oncoming energy futures are made. It is these decisions that will determine the quality of the new present, when it is being experienced and before it also disappears into the past.

The present is always based on our own 'now' energy view, and is our own specific and personal continuing mental exploration, or explanation, of what we are experiencing. It therefore provides continual comforting confirmation that, first, we exist as a 'physical' entity and, second, that we are the 'I' person who is going through the experience – see this, touch that, smell this, avoid this danger etc., and third, that we are a part of Mankind on an apparent physical Earth.

But no-one else sees our 'now' energy view in exactly the same way as we do, because their experience will depend on the way in which their Intellect interprets it in terms of their existence. There are minor differences between us but, of course, their experience of the same event will be very similar to our own and we can say that we share the same mental view of these experiences.

All of these views are correct for each of us and together help to make up the whole, thereby enabling all of us to share common experiences and make communal decisions. In accepting another's view, our Ego helps us to make 'allowances' for any slight differences.

Obviously, the other person's view is 'a bit wrong because he didn't see it/hear it properly' as we did and so on – but because, by and large, it's the same as our own view, it is acceptable and reassures us that it was a shared 'physical' experience and, therefore, that we are all physical beings together.

2. Past – Memory

However, in the very next instant or fraction of an instant, what we were experiencing as a 'present' energy image, is now a 'past' energy image and if it is considered of value, it might be filed away as a part of our memory. But it is constantly in danger of being pushed out of focus, or replaced, by a new 'now' mental image coming forward. This might be a part of a continuing mental energy sequence of events which together make up a story, or completely separate but loosely connected images.

We can say that the past is a reality which has gone, that is, it no longer appears real and it's only our ability to store and recall it as an energy image that makes us aware that it ever existed. The fact that others can also remember it, reinforces its apparent reality and adds to our physical group comfort. Apart from this, 'the reality' has vanished – only the energy image remains in memory.

Did it ever really physically exist? How do you know? Yes, I know that you can remember it, perhaps by associating the past with some particular object, but you need the mental energy image, within your memory, of that association for it to make sense in a relationship sort of a way.

But what if your memory is faulty in some way – you've lost a part of your past and it's the same as if you never had that experience. The specific energy content has been deleted. As far as you are concerned it never existed. How real was it if it can disappear so easily?

But regardless, even if your memory is sound, the experience no longer exists, except as a mental energy image or, if you like, as a 'piece' of mental energy filed away in a mental drawer. You can't bring it back as a real experience, only as a remembered energy experience with all its faults, so did it really ever exist? How do you know? But what if you only imagined it – you never really had the experience but your faulty memory insists that you did? Rather like a persistent dream causing a random energy image to be stored. You are stuck with an incorrect memory image.

So, how much reliance can we place on our memories to offer the right energy image? Normally, this isn't a problem, but you could experience similar energy convictions under hypnosis – we discussed this earlier. Your Intellect could be encouraged to generate a false energy image to be implanted in your mind. So, did the experience really happen? Who really knows? The point here is that we have to acknowledge that our evidence of reality can be fragile.

The ability to remember is critical to our living as an intelligent physical being, and the value of these past impressions is in their selective use to support the present 'here and now' knowledge of physical situations. It reassures us that we exist – we are here, we can remember – and it provides a basis on which new knowledge can be learned. That is, you have to have achieved a level of knowledge, at a particular instant, before you can fully understand any new knowledge that is likely to be apparent in the next instant.

It helps to provide our imagination with a basis to assist in judging the new 'now' energy experiences, and adds to or detracts from the basic judgment criteria used for continuing future selection – a sort of continuing information upgrader.

It is a normal, constant, but effortless process and requires the ability and willingness to continually give these matters a degree of consideration, using memory energy images of the past to assess how factual they are likely to be now, before proceeding into the future.

3. Future – Imagination

Similarly, until a future probable energy image is converted into a present energy image, the future only exists in imagination – that is, it's not real (whatever that means!). It is only a mental energy image of a number of future 'physical' possibilities, created by each individual according to the selection seen as appropriate to his wishes and circumstances, including the individual's past and present.

For example, you may have a number of future mental energy options available ranging from the barely possible, to the possible, and on to the probable, depending on your own particular and changing circumstances. As you proceed in the present, you are making decisions that will make these future options more or less likely, that is, the choice is narrowing – becoming more probable – until a selection is made, and this then becomes the new 'present' energy image, as you planned. This then influences a new lot of future energy images starting to appear in your imagination.

From a practical point of view, you may make arrangements for next week or next month (future), but because your circumstances have suddenly changed due to some unforeseen external factor, such as becoming involved in an accident, for example, the whole range of future impending options can immediately alter. These may now have to include a stay in hospital.

It's an endless choice depending on the variations caused by immediate circumstances, but it's all in the mind, that is, it's an energy image that is not yet real until you decide the pathway you are going to take. Then those particular mental energy images come forward to be converted into what is considered to be the required present 'real physical' image and so your life continues in that direction.

The choice you make of future options may place you in situations or circumstances that contain potential dangers, or influences, that may affect you. In recognising these, you rely on your memory of similar happenings in the past, to be reassured that you can handle whatever dangers may be apparent at that future time.

But keep in mind that we can't cover all possibilities. For example, we can guess, but we don't **know** what's going to happen to us in the very next instant or fraction of an instant, until it is a present experience, and there is only so much preventative action we can take to avoid problems.

The future, then, is constantly being shaped and reinforced to quite some degree by the present, but it is imaginary – a mental energy image that is unreal – until you choose it to be a present physical experience. But what converts it from an energy image into a 'real physical' experience? I can't answer that – it's an automatic mental process that occurs within the mind and tells us that we are now experiencing a specific physical reality. The acceptance of that reality then helps us to perpetuate the image of our own overall physicality.

The Importance of Memory

If the past no longer exists, except as a memory, and the future is yet to exist, isn't it reasonable to say that only the present is relevant, and it is our Intellect and memory which ties all of these concepts together to help in making sense of living in an apparent physical, ongoing 'now' world? We are aware of these images because we are geared to accept and process them in a particular way – that is, it is a part of our mental 'indoctrination' before birth, in order to live as a 'physical' being in a 'physical' world.

Your Intellect and your memory are of major importance in providing you with a 'reality' view. If you like, this provides you with a familiar 'starter backdrop' of situations, built up over the years, which you can use as a reference point for any new situations likely to come into view.

Consider the following encapsulation: imagination (Intellect) provides you with a mental selection of appropriate future energy options. At the instant that your Intellect acknowledges that a particular option is to be realised, one or more of these mental options are then translated into an apparent physical state, and you are able to experience it as a reality.

This satisfies your need for the new present 'reality' and then, when this need is exhausted, it subsequently moves the new reality into memory where it also remains as a past memory option to be remembered at will. The next following future option is then presented for processing and so the chain of events unfolds. There is a similarity to motion picture operation whereby a number of picture frames (stills) are sequentially displayed to provide the semblance of continuing motion.

We've already shown that our memories aren't really reliable interpreters of physical happenings, so if the appearance of reality depends on the ability of the mind to work (or interpret) in a special way, then how real is the physical world in which we live? Could I remind you again of the earlier comments about mental conditioning and of how hypnosis can alter the mind's perceptions?

Perhaps it also provides an explanation of why some people's view of the world is so disturbing that they are considered mad – their Intellect /memory only offers them a distorted translation of the world. Their conditioning is incomplete.

If we have no memory or concept of what has gone on before, then we are perpetually living in an uncertain and very alarming present moment, and the past (and time) has no meaning for us. The use of memory is critical in living in a physical world because it affects how we look at the present, by being able to constantly compare the present with the past to determine its familiarity and, therefore, our ability to handle whatever is in the present. Without this reference our very existence as an intelligent physical being is in doubt.

Dreams

Do we exist? If everything is energy then maybe we are 'schooled' into thinking of ourselves as real physical beings, but if true reality were known perhaps our lives could be a part of somebody else's dream. In the same way that we can apparently dream of all sorts of situations concerning an entity that is 'us', then maybe our lives are a figment of somebody else's mind.

So, how does dreaming fit into all of this? Taking this a bit slowly, I'm not sure if dreams are a manifestation of future or past options that did not materialise, or are products of the imagination, based on stories read of these times or maybe of other lives, or conversations with other people. But you may agree that a dream is an example – a very real and personal example – of a non-physical existence.

Regardless, it is reasonable to say that your mind makes these dream episodes seem real enough when you have them, so that dreams must have some origin that has access to your mind. Maybe dreams are a confused mixture of memory energy and imagination, sometimes resulting in frightening situations. In some instances, they can help in resolving present hidden conflicts, but may also be portents of things to come.

Dreams are a mental/audio visualisation that are interesting not only because of the subject at the time but, because we are asleep, it confirms the fact that, at that time, we don't need physical eyes to see and ears to hear, or limbs to move. We are experiencing sight, sound and movement from memory, or some other energy source.

But where do the images of nightmares and similar instances come from – as we are asleep, we are now processing, seeing and hearing apparent mental, visual and sound images of situations that are quite imaginary.

This suggests to me that it is reasonable to think that we will continue to need and use these energy faculties, seeing and hearing for example, as a part of our new spiritual lives after physical death, and also suggests that the transition will not be as difficult as we sometimes think. Our ability to understand our new situation will be supported by our new mental 'seeing' and 'hearing' abilities.

But doesn't the ability of the individual's Intellect to take a stored mental energy situation from its memory and make it seem real also establish the probability that all of Man's mental activities are just processes of energy and are only real to the extent that they are needed to support Man's illusion of his present and immediate physical existence?

So, as speculated in an earlier chapter, it seems to me that dreams are a forward view of our spiritual condition after physical death and confirm the point that, ultimately, we are all spiritual energy beings.

Thinking Energy

Now, is it too unreasonable to stretch 'ordinary' electromagnetic energy to include thinking energy? Not possible? Energy flow within the body can be measured so why not thinking energy as well? If it can be measured or quantified in some way, it has to be 'real'.

If this is so, then you may agree that my suggestion, that 'under some circumstances we are all energy beings', is reasonable. Perhaps a bit difficult to accept fully, but it remains a possibility until we find out for ourselves.

It might be helpful to also point out that a part of the Buddhist traditional teachings is to use meditation to cultivate the awareness of the separation of the mind and the physical body. This, to the point where it is acceptable that the body is no longer important, as it doesn't really physically exist, and only the Intellect/spirit continues on in its journey to its destiny. Isn't this much the same as has been suggested here?

This concept may be a bit difficult to grasp at first, and perhaps at this point the ability of the effects of hypnosis on the mind's perceptions could again be considered. Remember how easy it is to fool the mind into experiencing unreal situations? The mind's perceptions are largely based on life's experiences that, for the purpose of living, are regarded as reality, but even these can be altered, or reprogrammed if you like, by hypnosis, so that what the mind regards as reality can be fairly easily changed. The energy value in the mind's specific perception has been changed temporarily by hypnosis.

You may be familiar with the philosopher Descartes' definition of existence, 'I think, therefore, I am,' and it could be said that this is also pointing out that the thinking (energy) process sets the bounds by which the individual appears as a physical (or energy) being. The individual is being 'thought' into existence and every time that individual is encountered from then on, our memory energy image is updated. You will agree that our image of ourselves is constantly changing as we age or change our life experience. Isn't this further confirmation of the concept that Man is really an energy being?

Otherwise, it is being said that the thought is born of nothing, but it is also obvious that for a thought to be in existence requires that something or someone must think it. So, the ability to think requires the prior construct of a thinker and, therefore, as an apparent physical world was a part of the overall proposition, this also had to be 'thought into existence' and supports the concept that God is the original thinker.

We have also been given the gift of creative thinking – perhaps as a part of the test of Mankind's worthiness to exist. Since birth we have all been building a mental reference library to enable us to evaluate how to live in our physical environment. This alerts us to possible dangers – this is hard, this is soft, this is hot or cold, this is red/black, and so on – and as we grow older the reference library grows and becomes more detailed, and extended by education and experience.

These reference points are based on physical sensations of touch, smell, taste, hearing and sight, all of which cause electrical impulses to travel along nerve paths to our mind which, after processing them, stores them in our memory as electrical charges or impulses/waveforms of specific values.

So, the question arises again how real are the causes of these sensations if they are just stored electrical impulses. We can bring these memories back but they are no longer the physical entities we once thought they were. They are stored electrical impulses and if this is so, then how can we differentiate between what is 'real' and what is imagined?

They are both interpreted electrical impulses. Doesn't this support the point of view expressed earlier that those things we regard as physical 'hold in the hand' types of things may not really be so? How should this 'different thinking' affect us? Well, not at all, because as far as we are concerned, it is really just reinforcing the concept of the existence of a non- physical Self and may be considered a very reasonable point of view.

In a sort of scientific way, it's really providing a form of rationalisation of the human condition, as an 'energy' being and its relationships within an 'energy' world.

Wouldn't this still fit in with the scientific view that all matter consists of electrical charges and space? Think about that a bit more – maybe seeing and feeling isn't the infallible physical guide we think it is, but is acceptable because we are indoctrinated into not accepting any other concept than that of having a physical form!

Spiritual Man

We have discussed an alternative view of Physical Man and now need to look at two other energy forms that are also an inherent part of Mankind. These are Man's consciousness or Intellect, and his Inner Self that together are referred to as his Life Force. While these may be two different types of energy, they are interdependent and for convenience here, are regarded as one energy – spiritual energy.

However, while the existence or absence of Life Force can be confirmed, Science can't establish whether spiritual energy is a fact or not and this has to be a personal conviction based on the individual's inner consideration and instinct. A balance of probabilities.

Reports of spiritual visions have been documented down through the ages and it is suggested that the fact that some people have experienced these types of visions is because the range of their senses has been temporarily extended, at an emotional time, to accept an extra dimension of a spiritual energy kind. It is appreciated that this is not a very satisfactory answer, but is the best that can be offered at this time.

Similarly, this could be part of an explanation for 'near death' experiences. The person involved is experiencing a temporary and incomplete change from a physical existence to an energy existence, or at least is now more open to these energy influences before 'returning' back to life.

May I suggest, too, that this is a reasonable explanation of the resurrection of Jesus – at his death he was transformed into a spiritual energy form and subsequently appeared in this form to others. This does not deny any special abilities but confirms what happened and explains the absence of physical remains, while leaving unanswered the mystery of how this was achieved.

All a bit controversial, I know, but as this is also part of our physical living experience, it does provide an explanation for these puzzling effects and nudges us to accept the view that, just maybe, we are really spiritual beings, housed in an apparent physical body for the purpose of living in an apparent physical world.

It also provides further support for the comment made about God's lack of interest in Physical Man! If Man really only exists as an indestructible spirit, then God wouldn't need to be concerned about the results of physical matters that are illusory anyway. This is where, in the absence of absolute proof, a 'balance of probabilities' approach is justified and it is everybody's task to sit back and form their own opinion on what it all means to them.

Of course, you can ignore the whole subject if you wish, but remember, no-one else can or should make these decisions for you. If you wish to go along this path and are willing to accept another's possible errors, keeping in mind that religious viewpoints are also based on somebody's opinions centuries ago, then this is up to you.

But the way is open for you to look critically at your religious beliefs, your way of living and how you relate to your fellow man afresh, and perhaps with a bit of thought be more at peace with yourself than before. As always it's your choice.

Robert Rowe

CHAPTER ELEVEN

Summary

Well, this is the end of our discussion for now. We looked at our beliefs and questioned those that were a bit 'iffy', rejected quite a lot of the more obviously wrong items, and then endeavoured to establish who and what we are, on a more factual basis than previously. Where we had no facts we tried to reason our way into some unknown territory, using a 'balance of probabilities' approach.

It is reasonable to say that Science supports the concept that
a) Physical Man is Energy Man, and
b) his consciousness and Inner Self/Life Force are energy processes, and it may also be acceptable, on the balance of probability, that these form the ongoing spiritual energy known as the Soul.

Otherwise, the development of Mankind is pointless and Science's first task in this area of doubt is to produce suitable measuring devices to justify that when referring to spiritual energy and the scientist's energy, we are all speaking of the same thing but using different labels – energy used for different purposes and perhaps requiring different labels, but basically energy overall. At this point, the relationship between Philosophy and Science becomes very close and, you may agree, provides some justification for the statement that these are two ends of the same stick and that together they describe true reality.

This raises many questions including the following: Why does something exist instead of nothing? Why does order eventually develop out of chaos? What was there to start everything off on its journey? Why is our universe 'just right' for life to develop in the way that it has? Is there a specific reason for this or is this only one of a range of possibilities? Is there a multiplicity of universes in existence?

Does the universe have to support a life form in order to complete its formation and is the fact that we are here and are questioning these matters, proof that 'our' universe is becoming complete? And are our points of view biased because we are actually here and need to seek confirmation of why this is so to justify our existence (the need to know)?

Perhaps the real question of all that we have been discussing is this – how much reality are you prepared to accept in place of the unreality you have been encouraged to accept over the years? Only you can answer that one.

In brief, then, it is suggested that our journey can be made less confusing by acknowledging and accepting that:

1. Each of us is an individual, consisting of an apparent physical body designed to exist on Earth, which houses

    a) a life force plus an intelligent entity, the Intellect, to make this existence possible, and
    b) a spiritual entity, the Inner Self.

2. The common component to the universe and Man's existence is *ENERGY*, and that these three entities are types of energy that together represent the personality of the individual, and though quite separate in function, can and do on occasion interact together. Ultimately, they will become the ongoing Soul.

3. It may be that Man's true nature is as a spiritual energy being only, and that his physical appearance is primarily to facilitate his stay on Earth.

4. The progress of the individual's spirit on its journey whilst on Earth is quite independent of any and all man-made religions, and unaffected by religiously inspired guilt and bigotry.

5. Man has a direct relationship with all other living entities, and as the dominant earthly intelligent life form, has the responsibility of caring for the Earth and its inhabitants.

6. Man's physical life experiences are controlled by two factors – choice and chance.

7. While the body may die for whatever reason, Man's spirit is indestructible.

8. Man, by appealing to his Inner Self through meditation, can improve his health – both physically and mentally – but that this has to be based on an understanding that this can be achieved.

9. The purpose of Man's life on Earth is to enable his spirit to grow in knowledge so that in its next stage of development

(after physical death) it can, first, provide guidance to those remaining on Earth, and second, be ready to accept guidance on its way to a new life.

10. God is a supreme energy force that is indescribable and cannot be interpreted in human terms. A personal relationship with such a being requires the intelligence to take part in such an exchange, and is impossible until human spiritual development is at an appropriate stage.

11. It is a reasonable assumption, given that God has allowed Physical Man the freedom to do as he wishes with his world, that Man's physical problems are of little interest to God. This is shown by the fact that answers to these self-imposed problems have continued to elude Mankind over the centuries, despite prayers and pleas for these to be eased. But it is also a reasonable assumption that the human spirit is capable of providing answers to these problems and does so on occasion.

12. When referring to the absolute basic energy units of the universe, Science and Philosophy are referring to the same entity but using different names.

What Now?

So, how does this changed thinking affect us? Well, nothing has changed externally. We can still relate to our fellow man in the same way. We can enjoy the beauties of our world, nature, music and the arts generally, no matter what inspires them. It certainly doesn't mean that we can't appreciate the beauty of our churches and temples and use them for their true purposes – places of spiritual renewal.

God – a balance of probabilities?

But internally we now have the opportunity to base our lives on beliefs that include the wonders of a spiritual life and of God, and that are as factual and logical as we can make them, while leaving the door open for new truths as they are revealed. This has to be better than using beliefs which are largely static and unable to be substantiated today.

So, where do we go from here? Well, the first thing to do is to sort out how you feel about what has been said here. Does it seem a reasonable basis on which to have a fresh look at your own beliefs? If not, then try to see what is causing your doubts and give them the same critical thought that you have given what has been said here.

Remember that just because somebody held an opinion many years ago, doesn't necessarily make that opinion or viewpoint true today. Similarly, feeling comfortable about a traditional belief is not the same as being able to prove that that belief is true, and if it can't be proven to be true, shouldn't you look at it fairly critically regardless of the 'comfort' factor involved?

Another person's views that you can't reasonably confirm today are suspect and have no special claim for acceptance, apart from the immediate value that you are prepared to give them. As an average person you don't need a professional to tell you if something obvious is factual or not. You are quite able to decide, on your view of today's facts, what the best and most factual basis for living your life is. Of course, frequent changes in these views means that you haven't given sufficient thought or investigated these matters enough before you made your choice.

Keep in mind that differences of opinion about what has been written here are fine, as long as they are based on facts, or in the absence of facts, on a very strong probability factor.

<u>NOTE:</u> If your view of the facts doesn't support the comments made here and in previous pages, then you should disregard these comments in favour of whatever is factual to you. At least you should be more settled in your mind with whatever your beliefs are and that has to be a plus. However, from time to time you may find it advantageous to reread this book and give some further thought to those particular points to see whether they are still beyond question.

All you need is the willingness to explore these subjects as deeply as needed, until a conclusion that fits the available data comes to mind. Of course, you also need a critical Intellect that carefully tests these matters before changing your views. After all, as this is what you have been doing all your life about all sorts of things, why not about the most important part of your life as well?

It seems to me that, as always, there are choices to be made depending on how you feel about the proposed way forward. If you are content to continue to make your way unaided, then the pathway will unfold as you go, but you do need to persevere with the development of your own personal views. As has been stated earlier, these will change of their own accord as your needs change.

On the other hand, if you like to be a part of a group to explore options while still keeping your own needs in mind, then joining in with a suitable group is for you. Often the results from a group session are more concentrated than when working alone, but the danger here is that the group opinion may, with time, become a comfortable substitute for the 'less comfortable' individual search. Your quest becomes absorbed in the group 'whole' and your personal needs may not always be met.

Remember, nothing is final, this evaluation process never ceases. This is why you are reading these pages – you are seeking to re-evaluate your own philosophical point of view. But the need to change your views will decrease as the selection basis is made as complete as possible. Time is not a problem.

If you feel there is some substance to what has been said here, then you might like to look around you and join a group of like-minded people to see if there are discussion groups available that fill your particular needs.

Perhaps the Theosophical Society might be a good starting point. They are an international group and can usually point you to a contact for most needs. But be selective in what you decide to do and withdraw if you start to feel uneasy about something. You can always return if you wish at a later date.

Perhaps, as health is of primary interest to all, it might be beneficial if you were to join a holistic health care group, as these encourage discussions on physical, mental, spiritual and emotional wellbeing. All of these are interrelated and can be adopted or not, as you see fit and at your leisure.

These groups are usually nonsectarian, non-profit organisations and often include a wide range of professional health practitioners and laypeople in their make-up. Apart from an annual membership fee, there are no structured financial contribution arrangements and, importantly, they don't require a strict adherence to doctrinal matters of any sort.

Other Spiritual Quests

There are many practitioners who have investigated specialised exotic areas involving aspects of spirituality that you may also consider exploring, but keep in mind that these pathways are usually aimed at achieving specific results, which are not necessarily helpful. If care is not taken, an involvement can be quite distressing.

It may be considered worthwhile to try to achieve a clear understanding of the intended goal beforehand, rather than following a side issue that seems attractive for the moment. You may agree that a general spiritual approach to God as the provider of all spiritual energy might be preferable.

There is no one 'right way' and you should be able to select from a range of practices which suit your particular needs, keeping in mind that these will probably vary as you become more experienced in sorting them out. Usually, you will just become aware of a changed need, so take your time and proceed at your own pace. Always remember why you are doing this and assess any activity proposed to you with this in mind. If you feel your needs are not being answered, then reconsider the activity.

If you still feel unhappy about it, don't continue – there are always alternatives. It is pointless continuing with something that your Inner Self is telling you is not needed, but a change because something is uncomfortable, without determining why the discomfort exists, is a bit short-sighted, and should be avoided if you can.

If such a situation occurs, then rather than 'stew' over an apparently insoluble problem, I suggest you put it to one side for a period and try rereading relevant information to see if some clarification is already on hand. Perhaps it may help to read other works on the subject to get your mind working on other angles before you tackle it again. You will then probably feel better prepared for whatever decision you wish to make, but at all times you must be true to yourself.

If you are not a 'group joiner' then perhaps you could develop a program to suit your own needs. This is not too difficult if you think through what you are aiming at and set down a clear program of how this is to be achieved, although you should be open to change if this seems appropriate. Just keep to the basics and ensure that your goals are clear without conflict or contradictions. Again, time is not a problem, you can proceed at your own pace.

The practice of meditation, as a basis for your own holistic health care, is a good starter as this embodies basic principles for the relaxation of the mind and the wellbeing of the body. It can be practised by the individual in private, as is felt appropriate, and can also be used as a springboard to move into other disciplines as well.

Initially, why not attend a few classes to get the basics right while reading a few books on the subject to get a broad feel of the process. But at all times, be flexible in what you do. Listen to your innermost feelings and be prepared to change direction if you feel that there is a problem somewhere. Remember that only you will know if a change is required.

Finally, let me restate why all of these writings came about. I was dissatisfied with the abilities of the major religions to provide an adequate and reasonable explanation of their relevance, based on their historical activities and the problems that these have caused through the ages and are continuing to cause at this time. Despite all of this, they were still putting forward doctrines which, in my view, are really no longer tenable and are still causing great distress. This isn't good enough for me.

Once you are fairly clear about your own views, you may like to become involved in discussions with others about various aspects to further broaden your own understanding. But a word of caution. Remember that this type of discussion is tied in with basic emotions, and the apparent questioning of others' beliefs can be distressing to some people, so be gentle and allow room for others to also exist.

I am aware that some of what is contained here is confrontational, but not unrealistic given the facts as we see them today. So while I don't seek your acceptance of all that has been said, it is hoped that your views might have been clarified by the discussion and that you might also dare to be a bit different in thinking about the most important facts of your existence.

Afterthoughts

It should be understood that there is nothing new contained here, just a re-arrangement of existing thinking. My contribution is in discussing these to show how they are all interrelated. They are a part of the problems facing Mankind if the meaning of his existence and his future is to be clarified, and it is his responsibility to tackle it, or not, as he sees fit.

Something that struck me as interesting is the way in which circumstances seem to help out when most needed. This shouldn't surprise me because it's what I've been saying happens - but there's nothing like being proven correct.

The first example was at the time when I was considering what my next move should be, relative to surgery. I had also arrived at the stage where I was reaching some conclusions about what my beliefs should be. It suddenly occurred to me, on the way home from seeing the doctor, that if my beliefs had any validity, then I should be able to correct the problem by asking my Inner Self to assist in this process.

It was the *right answer* for my particular needs *at that time* on both counts, first, it meant that if successful, the decision about the need for surgery could be deferred maybe indefinitely, and second, it would prove to me that what I was putting forward in these writings was fairly correct or at least had some reasonable basis.

About 20 years has gone by without the need for surgery so it seems reasonable for me to at least claim that the problem has been held in abeyance by meditation and a half aspirin daily. Certainly, no-one can say that this is untrue – maybe, in their opinion, unlikely, but not untrue.

I also remember being somewhat sobered by the thought that this also was a part of the proof, for me, that God existed. If my Inner Self (Soul) existed, then I had to accept that a spirit world also must exist and that this must lead to the fact that God existed. How often are you able to be involved with a potential answer to a question of this importance?

The second example occurred later, at a time when I was experiencing some feelings of doubt and isolation. Having gone through the processes of trying to evolve a different way of looking at life by my own logic, I suddenly became very aware that I was opening myself up to all sorts of criticism from others, who were much better versed and more knowledgeable than I. Particularly from those who had been involved in study for many years in the areas I was seeking to criticise.

Surely, what was obvious to me should have been even more obvious to those who were professionals in these areas, and I wondered how my attempts at logic would stand up. As far as I knew at that time, nobody else seemed to have gone along the path I was following and I wondered why. Perhaps I had made a big mistake somewhere which the professionals had been able to avoid ... it's a very unsettling feeling to have.

Now, for a completely unconnected reason, I was exploring references about Oliver Cromwell, the Lord Protector of England who lived in the UK during the 1600s, and I came across a subsequent reference to Deism, a non-institutionalised form of religion which came into favour about 100 years later. I found that some of the views I've expressed here are very similar, in part, to those of the Deists, who included many notable thinkers of that day.

However, it has been valuable in that it has once again proven, as I suggested in the Introduction, that a layperson can sit down and, by applying his reason, arrive at an alternative philosophy of living that is more truthful and meaningful in this day and age than that offered to us by established religions.

No longer an unsettled feeling, but so much for reinventing the wheel and it is suggested that it would be worthwhile for the reader to conduct his own research into Deism and Theism at his leisure.

Stay well.

THE END

MEDITATION

Practical Considerations

1. Where?
At home, designate a quiet room (spare bedroom?) as the special place where you are going to meditate. This retreat should ideally be a quiet place where the blinds can be drawn to provide a comfortable measure of light control, generally a half-light is probably best. You will need a comfortable chair (not too comfortable as you may go to sleep!), but as you will be seated in it for perhaps up to about 30 minutes, it is pointless being unnecessarily uncomfortable.

It is important that you aren't interrupted during this time, as you need to concentrate your mind on the task at hand, so that you know that when you enter this room, at this particular time, you are automatically preparing yourself for a calming and self-awareness session and you know you won't be disturbed. If there is a particular need to be addressed, for example
'healing' or just a general 'time out' session, then this should become the focal point.

Others in the household should be aware of your special needs and their co-operation should be sought. Of course, there may be an occasion when an interruption is unavoidable, and if this is so, then just close off the session and attend to whatever is necessary, and pick it up again at the next session.

2. Session Time – How Long?

The amount of time to be spent at each session is quite variable and it may be worthwhile initially experimenting with this to suit yourself, but it is suggested that it will probably take about 10 minutes to settle yourself down and start to relax into a procedure which you will follow each time you enter into the session process.

You may find that overall about 30 minutes is sufficient but there is no hard and fast timetable to be observed and may vary according to the individual's needs and abilities. This time will pass fairly quickly. Certainly, less than about this time is probably insufficient, but remember, this is not a time trial – quality time is important, quantity time is not, and it is important that you don't 'push' yourself to the point where you are uncomfortable with what you are doing. Twice as long is not necessarily twice as beneficial.

Another point which you should keep in mind is that there may be times when you find yourself unable to settle and when this happens, then accept that, for whatever reason, it isn't appropriate just at that time to proceed and give it a miss – try again later.

3. How Often?

Generally speaking, this is left to the individual, but it is suggested that one session a day is probably the minimum and two sessions preferable. Time of day also seems to be up to the individual and you may like to sort out when it is best for you, that is, when there is a period of undisturbed time.

You may find that it seems easier at a particular time to relax into your meditation than other times and this will decide when you will conduct your session.

A session in the early morning and again at night before retiring, would probably be most suited to most people's needs, but make this a daily habit at these times, keeping in mind, the above point about 'quality time'.

Be curious about how the session unfolded and what was interesting about it – did you feel relaxed and at peace – if not, why not try to sort out what was not flowing properly and try to avoid it next time. There's no rigid right or wrong way, there's only the right way for you, so vary things to suit yourself within the context of a meditative session.

I found that the subject of meditation popped into my mind uninvited occasionally when gardening or when I had a quiet moment during the day, so at these times you may like to think and explore the concept a little.

4. So Let's Start a Session
So to begin, always enter your 'retreat' with the thought in mind that you are going to heal your body or ease some point of tension, just settle yourself in your chair and then, having relaxed your whole body processes, think about what you are trying to achieve in general terms and how you expect to achieve it. That is, you are seeking 'inner' help to overcome a serious health problem, or to achieve peace of mind, and that you need to be in touch with your Inner Self to gain this help. If it makes it easier, think of it as though you are preparing to have a mental conversation with another person.

God – a balance of probabilities?

It is understandable that the thought of consciously setting up a conversation with yourself about anything may seem a bit odd, but as this exercise involves a private attitude of mind, and is a formal statement to your Inner Self that you need its special healing assistance in a time of real need, it isn't unreasonable.

Sometimes it helps to satisfy the mind's incessant need to be doing something if you concentrate on listening to your breathing – perhaps at the throat, or at nostril levels – this helps it to avoid unwanted intrusive thoughts. You may like to reduce your breathing rate a little – this will probably happen anyway as you are seated at rest and can also have a calming influence generally.

If your mind wanders from 'listening' to your breathing then acknowledge that this is happening and purposely bring your mind back to your breathing – that is you are controlling what you are thinking about. This is no different to making a choice about thinking about any subject – something you do as a normal everyday activity.

Gradually you will find that listening to your breathing is quite normal and will lead to a
'calming of the mind', a stage when you can seek assistance for whatever your problem may be.

Remember, be comfortable with what you do – time is not a problem, so don't try to rush things – a ritualistic timetable approach doesn't help. Let it be something that happens to you in its own time. As a general guide, after perhaps 10–15 minutes of calmness and a gradual reduction in thought interruptions, you may experience 'seeing' wallpaper patterns and perhaps colours of various hues.

However, if you consciously try to see these mental effects, they usually disappear. You might like to develop the interesting trick of ignoring them while observing that they are there (yes, it can be done!).

These 'markers' may take quite a number of sessions to eventuate – it varies according to the person, but don't be discouraged about this aspect, as the general calming of the mind, in and of itself, is beneficial and is a part of what you are seeking. As a matter of interest, a blue/violet colour is usually an indicator of calmness, but don't 'work' at trying to turn blue – if it happens fine, enjoy the sensation, but if not then keep going anyway. Your priority is a condition of self-awareness, not to chase colours.

You should finish off each session by mentally expressing gratitude for any help given, and taking your time, start to slowly 'wake up' by moving your arms and legs a little and then opening your eyes. Spend a few minutes thinking and wondering about what occurred during the last 30 minutes or so. You are now ready for a good night's sleep, or if it's the morning, for the day's activities.

If you are a 'morning' person and normally awake at about 6.30 am, then without dressing, why not just take a rug with you to keep warm and go into your special room and spend a 'happy half-hour' before thinking of anything else. When the morning session is finished, then continue as normal – a cup of tea sounds good. Always try to feel confident that you are improving your health because you know you are enlisting the most powerful aid possible.

Keep in mind that: 1) your Inner Self will already 'know' of your problems because of its unique situation, and 2) there is no other way you can make such an intimate contact with your Inner Self except through your mind. The fact that you are doing this is a demonstration of spiritual development and is noteworthy in itself.

You can discuss this process at length, with others if you wish, but keep in mind that your experience may be somewhat meaningless to others, until it is a part of their personal experience too. You may find yourself thinking about these sessions at various times during the day and what you are experiencing during these times. If you can stop what you are doing and wonder about it all, then enjoy these odd moments. You could think of these 'in between bits' as helping to prepare you for the next session.

Seems too easy? Well, keep in mind that the hardest part is holding on to your belief that an improvement in your condition, or your outlook on life, can occur. You need to be absolutely single-minded about your belief that your condition is going to improve because of your contact with your Inner Self, and that you need to establish the program as an unvarying daily habit, for as long as it takes, to gain the required improvement in your outlook.

www.ingramcontent.com/pod-product-compliance
Lightning Source LLC
Chambersburg PA
CBHW071840230426
43671CB00012B/2019